S.P.C.K. THEOLOGICAL COLLECTIONS

Christ and the Younger Churches

THEOLOGICAL COLLECTIONS

I5

CHRIST
AND THE YOUNGER CHURCHES

THEOLOGICAL CONTRIBUTIONS
FROM
ASIA, AFRICA, AND LATIN AMERICA

José Miguez-Bonino
Adeolu Adegbola
Kosuke Koyama
John S. Mbiti
Choan-Seng Song
Kazo Kitamori
Mark Sunder Rao

EDITED WITH AN INTRODUCTION BY
Georg F. Vicedom

LONDON

S·P·C·K

1972

First published in Germany by
Chr. Kaiser Verlag München

First published in Great Britain in 1972
by S.P.C.K.
Holy Trinity Church
Marylebone Road
London, NW1 4DU

Printed in Great Britain by
Willmer Brothers Limited
Birkenhead

SBN 281 02477 4

CONTENTS

PUBLISHER'S NOTE

Written originally in a variety of languages (English, Spanish, Japanese) these essays were first collected into one volume by Professor Georg F. Vicedom and published in German translation by Kaiserverlag of Munich in the series *Theologische Stimmen aus Asien, Afrika, und Lateinamerika*. In the present volume the English contributions are in their original form and the others have been freshly translated into English.

CONTRIBUTORS

Georg F. Vicedom, D.Sc., D.D., is Professor of Mission and Religious Studies at the Augustana High School in Neuendettelsau.

José Miguez-Bonino, a Methodist; since 1954 Professor of Systematic Theology at the Buenos Aires Theological Seminary. He was an observer at Vatican II. His essay was written in Spanish and translated by Miss Margaret Lister.

Adeola Adegbola, a Methodist minister, Principal of Immanuel College, Ibadan, Nigeria. His essay is part of a lecture he gave at the All Africa Conference of Churches Inter-Church Aid in Enugu in 1965.

Kosuke Koyama, a Presbyterian, Principal of the Union Theological Seminary of South-East Asia; editor of the "South-East Asia Journal of Theology", in which his essay first appeared in English.

John S. Mbiti, an Anglican priest, who worked in an English parish at St Albans (1960–3); now Professor of Religious Studies at Makerere University College, Uganda. His essay is an original contribution written in English.

Choan-Seng Song, a Presbyterian, Principal of Tainan Theological College, Taiwan, Republic of China. His essay, written in Chinese, first appeared as an article in the "South-East Asia Journal of Theology".

Kazo Kitamori, a Lutheran; since 1943 Professor of Systematic Theology at the Japan Theological Seminary, which in 1949 received State recognition and became the Tokyo Union Seminary. His article originally written in Japanese, was translated by Raymond Hammer.

Mark Sunder Rao, the son of a Brahman, worked for a while as a journalist and is now on the staff of the Christian Institute for the Study of Religion and Society in Bangalore. His essay is part of his book *Ananyatva, Realization of Christian Non-Duality* (Bangalore, 1964).

CONTRIBUTORS

INTRODUCTION

GEORG F. VICEDOM

Conditioned by the missionary situation and the lack of academic theologians—a fact that especially John S. Mbiti points out— the proclamation of the faith demands that theological studies in Asia, Africa, and Latin America must be concerned with Biblical Theology. Theological reflections, on the other hand, or the attempt to fit the newly acquired knowledge into a system has always been a later result of theology. While the Churches on those continents still feel the missionary impulse, it goes without saying that they are interested in the encounter with the non-Christian religions, but not in the questions inherent in the Christian Faith. No wonder that Mbiti says that the Churches of Africa do not yet feel the need for theological questions. The so-called Younger Churches, too, must pass through the age of the "Apologists" before they in turn can become "Church Fathers". It seems that theological questions only arise when movements within the Church call for correction. Nevertheless, contributions to Christology were available in various journals, but they dealt mainly with the traditional questions.

In view of this situation, the original writings that had been asked for brought a certain surprise. In place of contributions to Christology others were received which were preoccupied with burning theological issues related to a particular area. Consequently the editors looked for a selection of already published papers. So, for instance, they added to the paper by José Miguez-Bonino one each from Africa and Asia. And they show how a genuine theology of history receives its proper direction only through the revelation of Jesus Christ. The studies of Christology published in this volume are at the same time confrontations with representatives of non-Christian religions who misrepresent the Christian message. We can tell from them how the so-called Younger Churches wrestle with synchretistic movements, an issue which becomes a matter of destiny for them. As one looks at synchretism on a world-wide scale one realizes that the saying is true today that the non-Christian religions become richer and more alive through synchretism whereas Christendom loses its power and authority when she allows herself to be drawn into it. The rejection of synchretism is a very hopeful sign, for we can tell from this where the Churches stand in their encounter with the world around them.

As to the motivation of the articles published in this volume, we can divide them into three groups. The first one starts with the question what assumptions we can make about the hearers of the Christian message so that they may be able to understand its teaching; or—putting it another way—How should we present it so that it is not alien to the people of a particular area? The contributions by John S. Mbiti and Mark Sunder Rao are concerned with this question, though in different ways. The former is aware of the given limitations of any assimilation, i.e. that which is new in the Christian message and cannot be surrendered. The latter, on the other hand, like his Roman Catholic colleague, Raimondo Panikkar[1], looks quite deliberately for a synthesis and wants to enrich the Christian faith by assimilating the Christian message to Indian structures of thought and piety. (After the publication of his paper "Ananyatva" this approach has led to a debate in India from which we include two comments. They show some of the questions that Rao's approach has provoked. The comments by Fr J. Britto Chethimattam and L. S. Rouner add a special note to this book because through them both an Indian Roman Catholic and an American Protestant theologian voice their views and so enable us to catch a glimpse of the theological debate within the Christian Church in India.)

In the second group of articles we see quite clearly the confrontation of the Christian faith with theological trends. It matters little for the moment whether these trends are found among the so-called reformed religions or within the Church. Choang-Seng Song devotes himself to the first category and thus renders an important service on behalf of theology. Alas, it is a sad fact that so far our theologians have hardly taken any notice of the extensive writings of Radhakrishnan and other reformed Hindus or Buddhists let alone studied them.[2] In view of what is happening in the non-Christian religions we should ask ourselves whether during this period of development the Younger Churches can avoid the "age of apologetics" which most of us tend to belittle. There are also signs that they will not be spared the influence of Gnosticism which, of course, will have its own shades of expression in different parts of the world. It stands to reason that theologians of the Younger Churches are bound to ask questions current in our Western theology. This is an important point both for our ecumenical outlook and our theology because the view is widespread that only our theology can help the Younger Churches. In this connection the work of Kosuke Koyama plays an important role. For here one can see how the thinking of Christians in Thailand is being influenced by the non-Christian background, and this probably without the fault of the Christian Missions. Koyama in his article on the "wrath of God" refers back to the Reformation and seeks to bring any super-ficial thinking on this subject face to face with the Christian mes-sage. In this respect he takes the same line as his fellow country-man, the great Japanese theologian Kazo Kitamori. He, too, in his "Theology of the Pain of God"[3] started with the Reformation and in his confrontation with Buddhism made one of the most original theological contributions in Asia. So it gives us great pleasure to include a further original article from him. When Kitamori talks about the pain of God he means that the wrath of God has been transformed by his love. Both these Japanese theologians are concerned with matters affecting their own environment as well as with contemporary theological issues. We can tell from their articles that the Younger Churches do not regard questions raised by the Reformation as old-fashioned and out-of-date, as we here in the West are sometimes given to understand.[4]

The third group of articles is concerned with the theme of God's activity in history and the theological problems raised by it. Koyama touches on it in his article. He sets himself against the "Pan-Causality" in Buddhism and also against their ideas of "apatheia" which has been taken over by the more pietistic Christians in Thailand. He also opposes the "monism of love" according to which the whole of history proceeds in perfect harmony. The contributions by José Miguez-Bonino and A. Adegbola take up especially the thesis—propounded in the West—that God is at work in the present historic development and that we discern the will of God in the political, social, and religious changes. They get on to a burning theological problem which has already been of central importance at ecumenical conferences.[5] This optimistic view of history, found also elsewhere, present the theologians of the Younger Churches with a great dilemma. God's providence and guidance are being employed for the affirmation of technical and social development. History becomes a second source of revelation, and the revelation that we find in Holy Scripture is dismissed as confined to a certain period in history. Jacques Rossel[6] describes very aptly the contradiction that theologians of the Younger Churches discern in this view of some Western theologians. "Over and over it is being repeated that both in its origin and its goal Western civilization is pagan, and in the same breath secularization, its most significant outcome, is being praised as though it were the kingdom of God. People are carried away be 'negritude', neo-Hinduism, and Zen-Buddhism, and at the same time they see the structure of the world of the future in a pluralistic, urbanized society." The peoples of Asia and Africa are split in two, which is a situation hardly appreciated by Western man. "They must explain to us why they reject Western civilization as a whole, yet accept its revolutions; why they make distinctions within Western history which appear remote to our Western contemporaries."[7] Since their ideal of life is different from ours statements such as the following—which admittedly were written with reference to natural theology—must seem very disturbing: "People like Harvey Cox and Arend van Leeuwen[8] who stress secularization have taken up a similar point of view though for different reasons. History—so we are told—is the biblical realm in which God is at work, and time and again nature is dismissed as the profane and desacralized sphere of purely empirical phenomena. God's activity in the Exodus and the Exile, in Jesus and the Church as well as in human history with its technical climax in the here and now can be regarded as the true object of God's revelation and design."[9] Such statements, however, cannot be justified theologically. They overlook not only the negative aspect of technical development which brings untold suffering to mankind, but also the problem of evil in general and man's striving after power. The logical conclusion would be that the development of communism as well as of the non-aligned nations comes under this concept of history. I want to illustrate how much theologians and laity of the Churches in Asia grapple with these questions by quoting a few sentences from a study group on "The theological basis for modernization by the Asian

Conference for Church and Society" which took place in the first half of October 1967 in Korea. "Although we believe in the impact that divine providence makes on the progress of history we doubt whether we can recognize God's activity in modernization or in any other event of history." "The process of modernization in our time compels us to look at the meaning of God's activity in the present history of Asia in the light of the reign of Jesus Christ over the world and of the fulfilment of all things through him. The first theological task of the Church is, therefore, to distinguish how in his creative providence God is at work in the process of modernization in judgment and in grace. It is only then that the Church can be obedient to him in each situation. The task of theology is, therefore, to work out a theology of history in which modernization can be seen within the context of the revelation of the final purpose that God has for man in Christ." "From this point of view, the role that man has and the responsibility that God has given to man in the shaping of the world cannot be overlooked. For this reason, modernization cannot be understood entirely in terms of the activity or the final goal of God, no more than in feudalism or in a planned democracy or in a free market economy." "Such a distinction is necessary if the processes of history are to be demythologized and taken seriously and if God's redeeming purposes and man's role in history are to be recognized."[10] If we do not pay attention to these critical questions there is the danger that it is only left for God to confirm man's history as this has happened for centuries in Islam.[11] These questions should be posed especially by those Churches which in the main see in their history an unalterable guide for the future.

Common to all contributions is the fact that they start from the revelation that is given in the Scriptures and go on from there to formulate their judgment. It is only in Rao's case that the Indian understanding of reality and truth sets up a tension between Scripture and tradition, and experienced reality is placed above objective teaching. As mentioned above, Rao has a definite missionary concern which his quotations of Kaj Baago bring out with even greater force. "Today's missionary task does not consist in calling men out of their religion in order to introduce them to another religion, but much more in leaving Christianity (as an organized religion) in order to penetrate into Hinduism or Buddhism. They are to be embraced as one's own religion provided it is not in conflict with Christ, and are to be regarded as the pre-condition, the background and the framework of the Christian Gospel in Asia."[12] It is, therefore, not a question of founding the Christian Church, but of making Christian Hindus or Buddhists. Adegbola regards as the decisive element of the historic revelation that God guides, judges and above all reigns. In Israel this reign is always traced back to God. So Adegbola raises the important question whether one can really say that all authority is of God, especially when it becomes clear that man's striving after power does not stop him from wrong and injustice in order to set up that reign. He, therefore, touches on the dark side of history in the same way as Miguez-Bonino, who speaks of the gloomy character of history, or like Koyama who speaks of the *opus alienum Dei*. These references make us realize that we hardly render a helpful service to the younger Churches if we offer them a harmonized view of history, either over-emphasizing the reign of Christ as in ecumenical circles, or through the monism of love which only knows of a "history without secrets". It is significant that Adegbola as a Methodist minister in trying to solve that problem arrives at a similar definition to the one that Werner Elert gave twenty years ago.[13] God reigns as Father in judgment and in mercy. Miguez-Bonino in his article starts off with the crucial question: "The acute problem is to define what he does and how one recognizes that he is at work. This is one of the most pressing questions facing theology today." He answers it by saying that in the Scriptures historic events are always interpreted prophetically. This interpretation, however, is not based on an ideology, but becomes revelation, and in this way is already a historic event in itself because it derives from the question to what extent men were obedient to God's overruling, or wanted to be obedient to it. For this reason, man's action in history can also be rejected. Now this leads to the commission of the Church. It is not for her to direct "God's world politics", but to interpret it. This is her prophetic function. The purpose of God in history, according to Miguez-Bonino, is complete redemption. But this is God's business. Christians can only participate in the creative and redeeming reign of God.

Now if this is the goal then redemption through Jesus Christ is the centre of history. Koyama makes a very profound statement when he points out that it is through his wrath and his judgement alone that God becomes the God of history. These actions of God in judgement and in mercy intervene in history, and is is only thus that history becomes history. It is then no more treated like a toy by the deity acting like a cycle as in India[14] or like an everlasting harmony as found in the East.[15] Rather, God is concerned with the salvation of man, and so salvation history takes place within world history. In view of the present theological debate about history Koyama refers to a significant word of Luther's that the God without the "strange work" is also the God with the "proper work". If God has nothing to do with salvation history then he may well be regarded as the *summum bonum*. Then he is available to man through mysticism and man can choose ethics as the path to redemption. This, however, say Kitamori, makes the impassibility of God a problem of history. For this would be the necessary inference of such an understanding of God. But then how can one speak of the hidden God and explain what is beyond human understanding in the development of history? Both contributions from Africa have something to say on that subject. John S. Mbiti speaks of the reality of demonic powers in very similar terms to those of the New Testament. The adherents of tribal religions may well have a knowledge of the casual coherence of things, and yet this does not provide an ultimate explanation. "The knowledge of natural causes is all the time shot through with the belief in supernatural powers to which vital importance is attached." Attempts are made to counteract these powers through magic in order to influence the course of events. "What is essential in things and actions is not what can be perceived with the senses, but something invisible that partakes of the supernatural sphere of power."[16] Religious traditions offered no help or prospect of the future to Africans. Hence Mbiti's strong emphasis on the "Christus Victor" theme which speaks of the one who intervenes as Saviour and Redeemer in the life of the African. Mbiti's emphasis is far from any *theologia gloriae*. He simply wants to point out what Jesus Christ means to the African. He is the other reality, not "something other", but "the other".[17] This can be seen in the fact that both Adegbola and Mbiti stress the resurrection of Christ as the decisive new event in history. For the first time this has opened up to the African a view into the future. Their history has been given a vision and a goal. Because of this, Adegbola believes that the Christian understanding of history must be grounded in the resurrection. He expresses very much the same view as Ulrich Wilkens: "The significance of Christ's resurrection as God's final self-revelation was that it set

B

in motion a process that would find its world-wide ratification in the course of the universal history of mankind. This was the basis for Paul's missionary work whereby in one single generation the Christian tradition established itself throughout the whole world. It was on this basis that all the historically conditioned forces of heathenism were so energetically and eagerly absorbed into the practice and theology of the early Church."[18] Thus Christ receives a central place in history.

A number of christological questions have already been referred to in these expositions so that the christological contributions fit into a coherent pattern. This confirms what Song says: "The history of Christian thought begins with, is held in tension all the way through by, and will be rejuvenated by the Christological problem." "... ultimately, all religious problems seem to come back to the one central point, i.e. the person and the work of the Christian Redeemer, Jesus Christ." Over against the other religions it accounts to the unique fact that they can claim universal validity for their teaching, but not for the founders of their religions. Like other human beings, these are subject to the law of reincarnation and Karma, and, therefore, cannot prove any specific redemption. With Jesus Christ, however, this is given. He is both true man and also true God and, unlike man, he is the only one whose relation with God was not broken, whereas all other men are subject to the fact that theirs was broken. Now in Jesus Christ somebody confronts them who in all things was like them and yet knew no sin. Mbiti underlines this point very strongly. Through the incarnation Jesus has become man's brother. This is why he can be the representative and mediator for man. This idea is of great importance for every Christian who has come out of the tribal religions. Where matriarchy is the rule, it is always the mother's brother who represents the whole family. But also where other customs exist it is always the elder brother who represents his kith and kin. Mbiti claims that Jesus has come into human society with all the qualifications that are required by the African. This legal and social cohesion is certainly significant. It means that every member of the community belongs to Jesus. For those who belong to tribal religions community is always a saving community. Our Western minds shrink from these implications of the incarnation and our theologians would delegate such an inference to natural theology. But we do not narrow down the implications of the incarnation by our concept of personality? "After all, God has not redeemed us through the word that has sounded from the heights of heaven, but through the word that has become flesh and that has come into this ordinary world in all its glory whose only evidence of truth is that it freely awaits its recognition."[19] Now Song tells us: "One of the profoundest ironies in the history of mankind is that when Jesus Christ, the Son of God, has taken upon himself our humanity on account of our salvation, he is constantly rejected as the Saviour of the world on the ground of that very humanity". The reasons for this vary. As true man and true God Jesus questions all the time our ideas of God, man, and the world. He tears man away from that relation with God that man has invented and confronts him with the real God. This is the greatest contrast to the Eastern religions, but also to the many images of God in our time. Our broken relationship with God can only be put right when we reorientate ourselves towards God. Forgiveness through God is only possible where man sees himself as creature and lets God be God. Forgiveness presupposes the "I-Thou" relationship. According to Kitamori, however, the basic problem in man's understanding of God is that in the person of Jesus Christ the idea of Lordship has been fused with the suffering of Christ. The natural man, of course, does not know a suffering God. Here is the uniqueness of Christ in relation to the other religions. And here we come up against the fundamental problem of Christology. At the end of his paper Song makes the same point when he speaks of "pain-love" for which the Chinese language has a word, but which has not been realized in the Chinese religion. In Jesus Christ this has become embodied in his person.

Vis-à-vis the non-Christian religions we face a tremendous problem here. I am wondering whether Mbiti's remark is true that the Cross causes no offence to the African. It might be possible that he has not yet discovered the secret of the Cross. Song comes closest to these questions when he states that Jesus Christ cannot be comprehended at all if we pull apart the person and the work of Jesus. This is what the Reform-Hindus do and also some of our theologians. Just as in Jesus the two natures form a unity so also person and work are united in him. "A christological question which is put from man's side by separating the Being and Act of Jesus Christ is condemned to miss its aim and to prove irrelevant." Basically, it amounts to playing with the question because on a purely abstract and neutral level it cannot be explained what Jesus was and what he did. When Song describes this unity he uses the terms Being and Act. Song is anxious to avoid any separation of Christology and Soteriology. The Cross without the person of Jesus would be meaningless for men. The same would apply if one could not say what the person of Jesus Christ had done for man's salvation. Song maintains, therefore, that Christology cannot be an abstract "locus" in Christian dogma, but that it must be dynamic. It cannot give a definition of the person and work of Christ if man cannot say at the same time what Christ means to him. "If the gospel is to make sense to African peoples it can happen only through their picture and experience of Jesus." (Mbiti.) This latter is the only one who in this connexion points out the importance of the sacraments which unite Christ with his own people. Rao, on the other hand, who argues that the mystical union is also permitted and possible for the Christian, does not seem to consider the Sacraments. He attempts rather to transfer to men the relationship within the Trinity and the relationship of the two natures of Christ to each other. He thinks that through the indwelling of the Holy Spirit the immanent indwelling of God in man is vouchsafed. We must not reject this attempt of presenting his case, but realize that here we get to the very core of Indian piety. We must really think through how God's relationship to men takes place in concrete terms. This question has been sadly neglected in Protestant theology.

In the different papers a number of questions—partly quite pointed ones—have been addressed to our theologians without mentioning them by name. It remains to be seen whether they are willing to take questions that theologians from the Younger Churches ask as seriously as when they come from the West. Since these questions from the Younger Churches arise out of their encounter with non-Christian religions they should be of particular relevance in so far as they affect the accuracy and universal validity of our theological statements. If they were taken seriously then our theology would also prove a help in the spread of the gospel and in the service of the Younger Churches. A theology would then come into being which is ecumenically orientated. This, in turn, would have its bearing on every theological statement which, after all, it should if it is to have a legitimate place within the Church of Jesus Christ.

I

HOW DOES GOD
ACT IN HISTORY?

JOSÉ MIGUEZ-BONINO

One of the most acute problems confronting contemporary theology is that of the nature, and the discerning, of God's action in history. In various ways and arising out of different contexts, it has been forced upon the World Council of Churches and upon the theologians of the various denominations as a theme of enquiry. Roman Catholic theology has devoted serious consideration to this problem, and the theme recurs repeatedly in the documents of the Second Vatican Council (particularly in the pastoral Constitution *Gaudium et spes*).

In South America, a number of factors serve to aggravate the problem:

1. Latin America is increasingly conscious of its place in history, through an awareness of its political, social, and economic situation within the framework of the tensions and groupings of the international scene. It is in these terms that the problem of the meaning and, deeper still, the creation and transformation of historical existence is presented.

2. In such a situation, the various ideologies offer their "key" to history and its goal, and at the same time offer a means of changing both the course and the goal of history. In the face of this challenge, some Christians tend to shrink from any confrontation between the Christian faith and the problem of history, taking refuge in a purely religious individualism, while others find a facile solution in identifying the Christian faith with the solutions offered by these ideologies: on the one hand reducing the Christian message to principles which are compatible with those put forward by the ideologies, and on the other equating history itself with a "second source of revelation".

3. But quite apart from the challenge of the ideologies, the faith carries within it an imperative which impels towards the quest for an ethic which will be both true to the Gospel and relevant to the present situation. Under these circumstances, it is impossible to escape from the problem of the meaning of history in relation to the Kingdom—a problem increasing in urgency as the need for a solution grows. The task is made yet more urgent and difficult by the strongly individualist message of most of the evangelicals, and the presence of the eschatological element, either as an individual and purely other-wordly hope, or as apocalypticism completely unrelated to history.

As much in Protestantism as in Roman Catholicism, this preoccupation with the meaning and interpretation of history has assumed an increasingly important place in the new pattern of theology in South America. This is evidenced on the Protestant side by the "Church and Society in Latin America" movement (ISAL). Here the thesis of the North American theologian, Paul Lehmann, has had a decisive influence: the purpose of God in history is "to make and keep man's life human".[1] Richard Shaull, the influential theologian and former missionary in Brazil, has moved in the same direction in considering the Latin American situation, in his development of a "theology of revolution".[2] The risk inherent in such a line of reasoning is apparent: the "human character" of life tends to be defined in terms of the standards, ideals, and values of a given moment in time, and thus indirectly history itself becomes a second source, and ultimately the definite source, of knowledge of God's will and of understanding of his action.

Curiously enough, following in a different line of theological and philosophical thought, some recent Roman Catholic theology is moving along a parallel course. Here Teilhard de Chardin, undoubtedly the most influential figure in Catholic theological thought concerned with the social transformation, provides the norm with his monist view of the universe and of history. A recent review defined his basic hypotheses as follows:

We believe that since Pentecost the Spirit is present in history;
We believe that God speaks to us through events;
We believe that events require interpretation;
We believe that light for that interpretation is in all flesh since the day of Pentecost;

We believe that the key to the interpretation of history and of each individual event lies in the mystery of death and resurrection;
We are in a world which dies and is brought to life again;
We and the things about us die and are brought to life again.

A few paragraphs later, Father Jorge Pascale summarizes the underlying philosophical premise: "The historical dimensions of the modern consciousness we have sketched should extend to incorporate in that consciousness the conviction that *this transformation of the world is in itself a divine transformation of human history.*" (our italics).[3]

It is in the context of this challenge and these considerations that we submit these theses, simply as a call to the discussion of this theme.

THESIS I

Neither the reality nor the manner of God's action in history can be established other than on the basis of the self-revelation of its purpose, compass, and meaning, evidenced in biblical history, as proclaimed to us in that same prophetic and apostolic testimony, with its pivotal centre in Jesus Christ.

This means that we cannot establish either a general philosophy of history based on an analysis of history itself, or a "Christian interpretation of history" which attempts to determine the nature and purpose of God's action in history in the way in which the prophets and apostles did so, in the light of the historical events to which they relate. Strictly speaking, we know how God acted only in those cases to which the Scriptures bear witness. Beyond this, we have only our interpretation based on those events, and this falls into an entirely different and ambiguous category, only analogically comparable to the first. Confusion of these two planes is a danger always latent in the Church's thinking. At doctrinal level, the Reformers recognized this danger when they refused to accept tradition as an authority of equal value with the Scriptures. On the ethico-political plane, it was recognized by the Barmen Declaration when it excluded the race or people as a source of revelation. But this temptation assumes many and varied forms, and must be constantly combatted.

THESIS II

The boundaries of God's action are those of history in its entirety in time and space, within which God works according to a divine plan to establish his universal reign.

Here we must distinguish three elements which are indispensable to our theme, and which must be studied in detail.

1. The universal nature of the field of the divine action and purpose: we are constantly reminded of this emphasis in the Scriptures by references to "many", "all", "whatsoever", "every one", in relation to the scope of Christ's work. Other texts refer to the "abundance" and the "multitudes" of people embraced by the purpose of God.

Theories of a "limited expiation", devised to underpin the affirmation of the sovereignty and freedom of grace, in fact deny that sovereignty by obscuring this aspect of biblical testimony. More serious to our present considerations, however, is its virtual rejection by fundamentalist movements, which in effect, restrict the action of God to the congregation of believers, consigning "secular" history in its entirety to the "power of the evil one". This attitude finds theological expression in a number of ways: in a pietistical withdrawal which does not deny in principle the universal sovereignty of God in history, but which derives no meaningful ethical conclusion from its acknowledgement of this; or by a strict separation of the scope of God's action in universal history from Christ's work, completely divorcing providence from redemption; or by a rigid apocalypticism, in which Christ's sole function is that of judge at the consummation of human history. These positions are only rarely presented in a considered theological form, but they constitute in effect the theological premisses on which the life, worship, structure, and "ethos" of these churches is based.

2. The *structure* of divine action follows a plan which presupposes distinct "times" and distinct "methods" of action. Recognition of this fact—the reflection of the biblical affirmation of a "living God"—frees us from the temptation of seeking to establish a "pattern of procedure" for God's action, by which we ultimately substitute for the expectation of God's action, our own conception of the means of divine intervention. This undoubtedly is the theological error which underlies allegorical interpretations of Scripture.

3. At the same time, we must ask ourselves whether there does not exist a certain constancy in God's "ways of acting"—not "standards" but "types" or "structures" of action. In this context it is useful to examine in detail the observations which Oscar Cullman has made on "representativeness" or vicariousness (God acting in and with a group as a whole), and "temporality" (the definitive character, the "once and for all", of certain times and periods).

The action of God, therefore, cannot be interpreted as a series of examples of the same behaviour; it must be interpreted in its dynamic. Every epoch has its own peculiar link with the Kingdom, its own "key", through which any understanding of that epoch must be sought. Thus in any interpretation of our history, it must be set, schematically speaking, within the "age of the Church": the era of the Church in the world and for the world, between the Resurrection and the Parousia. (See Thesis VI).

THESIS III

God works through the dynamic of historical events, without either suspending or eliminationg its categories, but assimilating them into his creating and redeeming purpose.

God's action does not constitute an ultra-history, one superimposed on the pattern of human events and of a different substance from human history: it is made from the same material. God's freedom in history does not operate as a freedom to annul the processes of history, but by using these same processes imprints on history a new meaning and direction, integrating the selfsame events into a creative context. The freedom of God does not destroy the historical order, but rather, to use a metaphor, encompasses it, preventing us from imprisoning ourselves irremediably within it.

The problem of how divine and human action inter-relate in history is an eternal theological problem. We must contend with opposition from two sources—different, yet curiously enough, related.

On the one hand, we are faced by those who construct a history of the Church and of the faithful which is divorced from the normal interplay of historical events: a history consisting entirely of miraculous happenings and the abrogation of intra-historical casualties. (There are histories of the mission field completely untrammelled by the mesh of international history of which they form a part.) Whether this emerges as Roman Catholic triumphalism or fundamentalist pietism, the result is the same: the inability to understand either secular history (which is seen as self-contained and separate), or the history of the Church.

On the other hand, there are those who acknowledge that the history of the Church is subject, as is Biblical history, to the same causalities, tensions, and processes as all history, but who see this as a closed process, imprisoned in an economic pan-causality. Consequently, they reject all possibility of "renewal" either inside or outside the Church, except through those crises which this determinism pronounces inevitable. What the adherents of this ideology do not realize is that its subjugation of history to a dogma disables them, as much as the fundamentalist-pietists against whom they are reacting, from accepting the variety and complexity of history itself. Whatever the theological standpoint from which the problem is viewed, it is essential on the one hand not to reduce the reality of the action, the historical "gesta", to a meaningless game of platonic shadows or a puppet-show, and on the other not to impeach the sovereign nature of divine intervention *in that same history*.

THESIS IV

Scriptural evidence of God's action is found in the interlocking of historical fact and prophetic witness to form a whole so closely knit that it becomes impossible to present the historical fact as a mere "brute fact" or the prophetic interpretation as a general principle, unrelated to the situation from which it arose.

Both the Old Testament and the New Testament are basically an account of events which are placed firmly in the context of human history and geography, events which are component parts of general history, the history of culture, and the history of religion; events, moreover, transmitted, elaborated, and recounted by the traditional means current at that time and indigenous to that environment. The Bible nevertheless recounts these events in the context of a prophetic interpretation, and they are presented prophetically (the Exodus from Egypt, the Fall of Babylon, or the Expansion of the Church). This prophetic interpretation itself constitutes an integral part of that event—so much so that the Bible does not hesitate to say that the "word of God" delivered by the prophet "brought about" this or that event. Yet this prophetic interpretation is not a human faculty, a discerning "vision", but a specific revelation by God: the Word "comes" to the prophet in relation to a particular situation.

1. We cannot attempt to apply to all historical events, nor to the whole of Church history, this prophetic charisma, which, strictly speaking, reaches its conclusion in the "history of salvation" attested by Scripture.

2. Neither can we use these prophetic interpretations directly as principles of historical interpretation applicable to history as a whole: this would be to disregard the unique nature of the history of salvation.

3 Nevertheless, in a subordinate sense, and on the basis of biblical evidence, we can recognize a prophetic function for the Church, relating to events both within and without the Church itself.

In those sectors of the ecumenical movement particularly concerned with the Church's responsibility in society, and in our own continent of South America—in both Roman Catholic and Protestant Churches—it has recently become the custom to speak of a "prophetic function of the Church" or of the Christian. This vocation consists in indicating the theological significance of historical events, particularly in the political and social field, and is based on that of the prophets, whose mission it was to "discern" what God was doing in the pattern of historical events. This facile use of the prophetic paradigm overlooks the fact that the differentiating factor between the true and the false prophet —for the latter also "discerns" divine action in the same events— is that the first "has received" the "word" from God, while the second has invented it. The Old Testament condemnation of the "self-appointed" prophet who "speaks the deceits of his own heart" is particularly severe.[4] Jorge V. Pixley, the Old Testament scholar from Nicaragua,[5] seems to suggest that the biblical doctrines of "justice" and "the Covenant" can be seen as channels of the prophetic interpretation of God's personal and active intervention then and now.

In the context of this close and inextricable intertwining of historical event and prophetic interpretation, James Barr's protest against a one-sided understanding of revelation deserves our attention[6]: he rejects this conception of revelation exclusively as a historical "gesture", which reduces that theological consideration which we find in the Bible itself as the context and interpretaion of that history to a secondary and merely interpretative—to certain extent less important—role, more human and less divine. This does not, however, commit us to drawing the same conclusions as the author deduces from his observations.

THESIS V

In the sense of the previous thesis, and completing it, we affirm that the action of God in history is universal and permeates history with its dynamic; but its meaning is discernible only by faith, within the limits of perception prevailing in the "age of the Church" in which we live.

1. To faith, every historical event is an act of God, which fulfils, often *sub specie contraria*, the redeeming and restoring purpose of God, shown forth and accomplished in Jesus.

2. Faith, nevertheless, has no plan or interpretation of those events which permits of their being fitted harmoniously into a philosophy of history: it often stands confused and lost in the maze of historical events. The vision of faith in the era preceeding the ultimate "apocalypse" is the vision of a mystery: the mysterious working of God's grace within the structure of the old "era".

It is necessary to emphasize this precariousness of the vision of faith in the face of the tendency of both Catholic and Protestant theology to integrate the vision of faith in an optimistic historical and philosophical perspective in which contradictory signs are dismissed as simply transitory phenomena to be superseded by the "dynamic of history" or by the "process of evolution", which are identified with the divine purpose. This transforms faith into a philosophy which in its turn becomes the foundation of unequivocal action, a new certainty which springs not, as in the case of pietism, from an inner experience, but from a mystique of progress or of evolution.

3. Nevertheless, faith is given signs, i.e. glimpses of the meaning of God's action in the world, based on what we know of God's action in the history of salvation. In this sense, but this only, the Church and the believer can venture to offer a prophetic witness

related to what occurs in the world, and to act accordingly. But this witness and action are in no way justified in themselves or in relation to any infallible standard of interpretation of the action of God: they are purely provisional, fallible, and temporary, and can only be offered under the promise of forgiveness of sin (hence the impossibility of a Christian "politics", "economy", "ideology", or "programme".)

4. When we ask ourselves if it is possible for us, in this limited and tentative way, to glimpse the meaning of God's action in history, we can discern a direction in the action of God apparent in the Scriptures, namely the redemption of human life in its totality (individual and communal, spiritual and physical, present and future). That redemption is described in terms drawn from everyday human experience which, although they have a special significance in their biblical context, permit of a certain analogous projection in secular history (insofar as God's action opens the way for, and makes possible, a human action). A projection of these terms (basically: reconciliation, justice, peace, liberation), and the biblical paradigms in which they are used, allows the believer to orientate himself in his search in and through faith, for his course of conduct in the *civita terrena*. But we must not forget that we are here presented not with general principles or concepts, but with a certain direction, a "way" which the Christian seeks, that will provide not so much a coherent explanation of things, as a means of expressing in a responsible form, and within the pattern of history, his service to his neighbour. In any case, this discernment crystallizes in the decision of faith, which in the last analysis does not seek any justification beyond itself, but is justified solely in the light of God's grace.

This then is the task—the very limited and penultimate task —of theological ethics: to perfect the instruments of theological analysis of biblical testimony, and to define the conditions which make possible its "parabolic" projection, indirectly and in an intermediary role, into the contemporary situation.

5. Theologically speaking, it is important to point out that this function we have spoken of can be fulfilled within the limitations of the perception of faith, not because we find in the redemptive work of God in Christ an "open sesame", a sort of secret code by which we can discover the will of God, or create a sacred philosophy of history, thus reintroducing what we had previously rejected; rather, this uncertain power of discerning through faith

has it roots in Christ, whom it acknowledges as One who transforms, renews, and reshapes history, and who has placed us
within it. Therefore, it is more important that the believers "are"
the history of God in the world, than that they should engage in
the equivocal task of interpreting that history. In the last analysis,
the histories of Israel and of Christ do not explain the meaning
of history: they create it. It is on this belief that the life of the
Church is founded.

THESIS VI

*The particular relationship between our era and the Kingdom (cf
Theses II and V) is determined by its position in time between the
Crucifixion and the Resurrection of Christ on the one hand, and
the Parousia on the other. Consequently God's action in that era
will share their "veiled" nature, and at the same time carry the
signs of the end and anticipation of the final consummation.*

1. That veiled quality relates not only to the sphere of recognition
(Thesis V [1]) but can take the concrete form of tension,
contradiction, and conflict. The power of God is revealed in
impotence; glory is revealed in the Cross. Triumph is visible only
to the eye of faith. The witness of the Church in the world
assumes the form of martyrdom.

2. The total correspondence of love and power, which character-
izes the final "unveiled" action of God, is refracted in the history
in which we still live, projecting a sector of violence. In other
words, in our era, in which evil exists although it does not rule,
ends and means are not harmonized and God subordinates the
interplay of ends and means in this world to his purpose, without
abrogating their characteristic ambiguity. Consequently, whatever
is achieved in this world, even by the Church, is by nature
provisional and temporary, and destined in time to be assimilated,
transformed, and surpassed by the Kingdom.

3. The nature of the Kingdom is nevertheless reflected too in the
history of this world: the structure of the Agape-based society
invades the societies whose foundation is Eros—as much through
the creative and sustaining acts of God as by the power of God in
the preaching of the Gospel. Insofar as it responds in faith and
obedience to the prompting of the Spirit which seeks to work
through it, the Church can in fact offer an interpretation of

history which becomes woven into the very web of history itself.

It is in the light of these affirmations that a profound consideration of the Church's responsibility becomes indispensable to the Christian ethic.

On the one hand, it seems to exclude any theocratic or ecclesiastical pretensions, whether these derive from the old aristocratic sources or from the new democratic or socialist sources: the Church has no perfect plan for society, nor is her action free of the ambivalence inherent in all human activity.

This is the basis of our objection to the—admittedly important —plans to bring about a "Christian revolution" in Latin America. On the other hand, it would equally exclude the serving of the life of the Christian community from the problems of the society in which it is set: in each the same contradiction is apparent; in each the redeeming power of Christ is at work; but there is a difference in the kind and perception of that action through the presence of the Spirit, and his testimony received in faith by Christ's people. In this way, it becomes possible for the Church to bear a sanctifying witness in society, which is relevant to society's present situation. This witness relates not only to the action born of faith of the individual Christian in the world, important though this is, but the very existence "in faith" of the congregation of believers.

Moreover, the Church interprets and creates history by the preaching of the Gospel, through which Christ himself is present in the world, requiring and making possible the obedience of faith: revealing to that obedience the mystery of his present and future sovereignty, and at the same time disclosing the source in which the Christian community has its being, and by which human history is sustained until its final consummation.

2

A CHRISTIAN INTERPRETATION
OF THE AFRICAN REVOLUTION

ADEOLU ADEGBOLA

At the inaugural Assembly of the All Africa Conference of Churches held in Kampala in April 1963, attempts were made to give a Christian interpretation of the African revolution and to relate the same to the parallel revolution which is going on within the life of the churches in Africa with a view to discovering the demands of freedom and unity which God is placing on the conscience of the African Christians in this generation. Note was taken of the changes taking place in the social, political, and economic life of the different countries as also of the growing autonomy of the African churches, the assumption of greater leadership responsibilities by African churchmen and the need for the Church further to be aware of itself and work towards greater freedom and unity in Christ in order to be able to witness to the African social revolution. Unfortunately, there have been many who regarded the voices at Kampala primarily as African effusions against missionaries and missionary societies and who have only tolerated the event as if to say "the Africans have brought out their tom-toms in Kampala and it is well we grant them the sound of their drum-beats". Others have suggested that there was more nationalism in Kampala than evangelism, and that this might not be a good omen for the future of the Church on this continent.

It is important for us as African Christians or as Christians who are vitally committed to the Christian mission on the African continent to engage with greater sincerity and earnestness in an interpretation of the times we live in, for this interpretation in itself is part of our Christian responsibility, apart from its value in making clear to us the direction and objectives of our future activities in the service of the people.

Let us make at least two points by way of summary of the feelings and viewponts expressed in Kampala. Firstly, it can be said that the African revolution is a harvest of Christian missions. I was asked not too long after Kampala by a non-African friend, "When will you Africans look at your situation more objectively and stop lashing out at missionaries?" I wonder, how otherwise can we look at our situation objectively except through an examination of the missionary endeavours among us? Our constant reference to the missionary past is an expression of our conviction that the missionary agencies among us (church, school, medical institutions, community development establishments, etc.) have been greatly used of God to bring Africa to its present position of honour and trust, and that the Church still has a unique part to play in the service of the nations. What has been a pity is that there is evidence to suggest that Christian mission in the past has not been clear or conscious enough about the relevance of its activities in relation to a prospective social revolution. The baby arrived and we have all been surprised to see what we have been carrying in the womb of missionary activities all the time. For Christian service in the future to be productive, it needs to be guided by a sympathetic understanding of the present course of events, and strengthened by the conviction that evangelism is bound to have social effects or even must be undergirded by direct social service.

There is as yet very little documentation on Christian social thought in the African Church, but there is ample evidence that the frustration which accompanies the rapidity of social change and its upsetting of the churches' social programme has led many to doubt whether the Church has any positive role in the new situation or whether the divine plan to make known "through the Church the manifold wisdom of God" should not be interpreted wholly in evangelistic terms. The missionary movement itself has previously explained its action in several ways which today are open to serious re-examination since the whole enterprise in Africa has come under severe attack for its alleged alignment and co-operation with the colonial subjugation of the indigenuous people, for its having allowed colonial policy to dictate the pace and hinder the extent of leadership training for Church and for society, for its lack of courage to speak out in condemnation of social evil and, when need be, play vicariously the role of the local prophet of doom towards the revivifying of the internal life of the Church itself which is no longer able to

c

sustain hope, inspire social action, and impart the traditional Christian qualities of holiness, purity, righteousness, and peace. The Church which grew out of that missionary endeavour today needs to seek ways of interpreting the social situation and of discovering new forms of service which the situation demands.

Since the Evanston Assembly of the World Council of Churches, a number of Rapid Social Change Studies have been made in Ghana, Cameroon, Liberia, the Copperbelt, Nigeria, Kenya, and Tanganyika (now Tanzania). These studies have introduced a new line in Christian social thinking in Africa, but they cannot yet be said to have made a significant impact on the social thinking of the Church. In the meantime, there is a lull and perplexed uncertaintly in the area of social activity in the life of the Church while governments are taking big strides to make up for time lost in community development and social progress. The dominant figures in the field of social thought and action in Africa today are the Governments and dedicated individuals.

Of the African Rapid Social Change Studies made during the past few years, only the Tanganyika study has so far given specific attention to the questions arising out of the background of pietistic theology which cast doubt on the justification of the involvement of the Christian community in the sociological changes of a country. The interim Report sees as the setting of the biblical drama of salvation the kaleidoscope of the changing life of the people of Israel in contact with the people to whom they were at one time subjected, and with others whom they were seeking to subjugate. The interesting parallel between the struggles of the people of Israel after centuries of their wandering in the wilderness of tribalism, colonialism, and exile, and the disrupting events which have featured the life of the African countries for more than a century, was not allowed to pass unnoticed. In the light of this, it was noted that the idea of a changing society is not new to the Bible, and that if we allow ourselves to be guided by biblical insight and not the subjective mood of our historical situation, we will have to recognize that the eschatological emphasis of the prophets and of the New Testament points to the perpetual occurrence of change until the time of the eschaton when all things will be fulfilled in Christ. "For we know that the whole creation groaneth and travaileth in pain together until now. And not only they, but ourselves also ... even we ourselves groan within ourselves...." (Rom. 8.22–3). The Christian therefore should not be so preoccupied by the passing changes as to forget the wider context in which the present changes are experienced.

The Tanzania Report goes on to relate the Christian concern for the "life to come" to his concern for the "life that now is", and indicates the need to correct the mistaken view by which the Christian concern for the world to come tends to lessen the importance of man's present existence rather than heighten its significance by showing it *sub specie aeternitatis*, not necessarily to produce a merely pietistic mood, but to bring about the responsible engagement of the Christian in doing the will of God "on earth as it is in heaven".

So, Evangelism as the task of the Church is not to be interpreted in the narrow sense of "saving souls", but in the wider and more practical sense of serving the world which God so loved that he gave his only begotten Son to serve it. And the incarnate life of the Son of God who came was lived constantly in costly service to which he in turn called his disciples. Thus, love and service to one's neighbour have become the proof of true Christian discipleship, and the word of approbation reserved for the blessed includes "Inasmuch as ye have done it unto the least of these, ye have done it unto me". In serving the people of the nation, the Church is serving her Servant Lord. "Worship, evangelism and service, these three elements constitute together our witness to Christ. Each stands in its own right and must be held together in the fellowship of the common life which the Holy Spirit creates. . . . Evangelism which does not spring out of the Church's common life and love expressed in service will become mere empty sound".

Secondly, the African revolution is a triumph of Christian ideals which have been taught and preached, worked for and fought for. Which of the changes in Africa cannot be traced back to the victory of justice and the restoration of human dignity? The concept of "African personality", for example, must be recognized as having its origin in the Christian conscience. It began as a protest against the assumption which later became a practical axiom by which the African was denied recognition as a living personality due for respect and for the full membership of developed civilized societies. The historical background includes the social patterns, the residual of which still exists in South Africa, Southern Rhodesia, and Portuguese territories in Africa. It is strange that those who once accepted and adopted the concept of the African as "a child race" today refuse to acknowledge the validity of the claim that Africa has now come of age, at least is coming of age. This is the concept of African personality. In so far as this concept stands for the principles of justice, the spiritual value of the human personality, self-respect, self-determination, freedom to develop to be the best which God permits and ordains each human being and each human society to be, moral responsibility etc., Christians therefore ought to hail it with gratitude and engage zealously in redefining it with Christian insight, humility, and hope. To render this service, we must be clear what moral and spiritual issues are involved in the current endeavours and to ensure the successful emergence of new moral dynamics for the strengthening of the nations.

For this reason, we would give encouragement to all attempts to evolve indigenous styles of facing social and political problems. It does not accord with national sovereignty and the spirit of self-determination with which the struggle for independence was fought should African nations continue endlessly to copy and ape systems carefully evolved in other parts of the world. Too much copying in the past has killed initiative and the power of creative imagination in African countries prior to the present era. It is therefore right that Africa should resist any further attempts from whatever quarters to pervert the sense of self-respect or raise doubt in the ability of the people to think, to originate, to produce, and to bring to maturity the systems and organizations which are now growing up here and there on the continent.

As Christians, we need to claim for the people the right to protect suitable traditional institutions and to encourage an adaptation of indigenous structures to fit them for the social and political realities of the twentieth century. Thus will the African gain the confidence which he needs for living in the emerging world community, and, if possible, to make some contribution directly and indirectly to the establishment of a peaceful and just coexistence of the nations of the world.

As Christians, we need to assert that since the people have known poverty, disease, and an exceedingly high rate of infantile mortality in the past, they now have justification for hoping that the era of political freedom and self-government should bring with it an appreciable measure of economic advantages. Christians in Africa should not tolerate any suggestion that this hope of the people that their standard of living should be raised is in any way due to immaturity, wrong expectations, lack of understanding of the values and demands of free enterprise, or even an

un-Christian coveting of the materialistic comforts of this techno-
logical generation. Rather, it may be urgent and imperative for
the Church in a number of countries to adopt the slogan
"Freedom and Work" not as a political stunt, but as a prophetic
injunction carrying the weight of biblical support and of
theological compulsion.

There seems to be a general agreement that the changing
patterns of life on the African scene have to be interpreted in
terms of divine activities and providential intervention. Christians
need to realize that a providential explanation of historical events
is not peculiarly Christian. In the contemporary African scene,
the view is shared by Muslims and pagans also. There is a grave
risk in adopting this interpretation therefore, simply because it is
a general, not necessarily Christian, point of view. Christians who
speak of providence must make sure that their belief does not
spring from the pagan background of interpreting inexplicable
historical events by reference to Fate or Destiny. The difference
between Fate and Providence depends largely upon the character
attributed to the divine power behind the event. It makes a
difference to think of "the God and Father of our Lord Jesus
Christ" as involved actively in contemporary social history.

Dr Charles Cochrane in his study entitled *Christianity and
Classical Culture* has traced the decline of the Roman Empire
to the "failure of the classical mind" to understand and appreciate
the meaning of change. They sought to explain it only in terms
either of uncontrollable Fate or of unpredictable Chance. Both
explanations failed to prepare and sustain men for the trying
experience and insecurity which change brought about. Dr
Cochrane adduced evidence to show that it was the Christian
Faith, as interpreted robustly by that great African theologian,
Augustine, and popularized by the Church of his day, which
released men from the paralysing sense of insecurity and liberated
new energies for responsible living. They found faith in Providence
and got excited with eagerness to discover God's next move in
his world.

Only as men see change today in the light of God's dynamic
activity in history making for righteousness will they be able to
rise and make their heritage sure. It is significant therefore that
the prevailing attitude of the Church as expressed in the message
of the All Africa Conference of Churches both in 1958 and 1963
and of the All Africa Christian Youth Assembly in 1962-3 is
"We rejoice in the political freedom of the people of our

continent. . . ." Indeed, if God is a God of history, a God who is known by his deeds, and whose purposes are realistic only through history, then change is inevitable. If God is he who judges, then Christians must always expect that he must intervene in history, and they must welcome his visitation with penitence, joy, hope, and obedience.

In spite of what we may think about ourselves as "makers of history", or such other self-congratulating phrases, mankind is pleased to use about itself at the crest of any human achievement, the Christian has to keep constantly in mind that it is God himself who is the architect and controller of history. The Christian has always to proclaim the sovereignty of Christ who brings changes about, we are his instruments; it is God who rules, we are his agents.

We are his his agents? But there are those who have similarly seen the providential and electionist hand of God in the raising up of colonial powers and their rule for good or ill over their subjects. This is the viewpoint proposed in the book *Caesar, the Beloved Enemy* by the great British missionary leader, Dr Max Warren of the Church Missionary Society in London.

His argument was that colonialism should not only be explained but also justified as part of "the purpose of God according to election" since in "the over-ruling providence of God" it has been an instrument of peace, progress, and God's goodwill in the world. It is necessary, therefore, to examine carefully this theological issue of God's action in history.

Prior to the question of how God rules in history is the biblical affirmation that he rules. God is conceived of in the Old Testament primarily as he who rules, the Lord, the King of glory, mighty in deeds. The record of the story of the beginning of political kingship among the Israelites indicates for us the prophetic attitude to the whole question of kingship and by which Israelite kingship was assessed and judged all their days. In the days of the "Judges", soon after the nomadic Hebrews got into Palestine, Gideon won his mighty victory over the Midianites (Judges 8), and the spontaneous demand of the people of Israel to him was "Rule thou over us, both thou and thy son, and thy son's son also: for thou has delivered us from the hand of the Midianites." But Gideon said unto them, "I will not rule over you, neither shall my son rule over you: the Lord shall rule over you". Thus, the first Israelite attempt to establish a monarchy was rebuffed on the ground that they already had a king. Yahweh was their king. In later days, whenever they had a disagreement with a king who had been anointed to rule over them in the name of the Lord, the prophet was not slow to invoke the kingship of God and the representative role of the earthly ruler (1 Sam. 8.7; 10.18–19

The idea is carried over into the New Testament. The gospel is not primarily a new teaching about a way of life, it is not a new philosophy. Rather, it is a proclamation that in Jesus Christ, God has himself achieved the fulfilment of his purpose for the world, his rule has triumphed over all, in him new creation has come into being, the new age has begun. The resurrection of Jesus was interpreted in the New Testament not only as victory over death, not only that Jesus rose from the dead because death could not have power over him, not only that he "being raised from the dead dieth no more; death hath no more dominion over him". The great proclamation of the resurrection which brought the Church into existence in Palestine and because of which it has had an impetus to spread to different parts of the world is the experienced inference of faith that in the resurrection God has intervened in the life of the world and has thereby brought his new creation into being.

He who said in the beginning "Let there be light" has in the resurrection of Jesus Christ proclaimed to the world "Behold, I make all things new". A new world is thus created, a new humanity, a new society, a completely new creation. From the point of view of the Christian, history has to be studied in the light of the resurrection, an event in which God himself has acted, an event which man could not have brought about but which God has executed in order to correct that which man has done, and perfect that which he himself has set out to accomplish.

In the light of the ressurection, therefore, a changed society, whenever and wherever it occurs, is not the work of man. It is the triumph of the power and grace of God. It is an occurrence in time and space whereby believers can declare that in truth "God hath visited and redeemed his people". But when God "visits", his visitation is known not only by the end result which is redemption. It is known also in the sometimes antecedent and at other times procedural act of judgment. The Son of God has come into the world not to judge the world, but that the world might be saved through him.

Yet, at the same time, the world to which he comes has been judged already, the society to which he comes is automatically judged because so much of the goodness of man is bound up with evil, perversion through self-will. That is why he has come. That is why he always comes, because of the perversion, in order to redeem the situation. But the very coming itself is a condemnation of the established order, in that man is made for light, and the children of men prefer darkness to light, generate darkness rather than light. The resurrection event rekindles the light and makes those who believe into children of light. The Christian must therefore live with the consciousness that he exists in the redeemed era of God and has to work for the eschatological era which God wills to bring about.

The Coronation Psalms (Psalms 93–100) got their name because they extolled the kingship of Yahweh and were probably used in the coronation of successive kings of Israel. At the coronation of their kings, the Israelites sang not the praise of earthly pontiffs, but the kingship and sovereignty of God. That is how it should be. Contemporary events, not only in the newer nations of Africa but also in many other parts of the world persuade our generations to wonder whether it can be said with Paul without any qualifications "For there is no power but of God: the powers that be are ordained of God" (Rom. 13.1). There are those who seize power for themselves by military coups or by direct assassination of political opponents. The moral invalidity of their case sometimes raises doubts in international circles as to the legal validity of their rule. Does this not sugeest that we should hesitate to identify the role of men in colonial or anti-colonial connections with the rule of God in history?

If elections are rigged, if voters are deliberately hoodwinked by a few in the privileged position of having a smattering of education, or if the electorate is corruptly seduced by a liberal distribution of largesse at election times, if a few violently seize power by a military *coup d'état*, or if others return to power through successful staging of counter-revolutions or a careful manipulation of international political forces, would it not be a misuse of biblical texts to base the authority to rule on the suggestion that all authority is ordained of God? Those who asume political power by military might should confess that they intend to rule by force, and those who gain or retain power by dishonest means should own with penitence that they have lost confidence in the ultimate triumph of righteousness and have allied themselves with the princes of darkness.

There is certainly an ambiguity about the role of human agents

in history. They may be established and used of God or they
may be self-created and become an instrument of sin. The paradox
in human kingship raises the paradox in divine kingship. Human
rulers are under orders. Divine kingship is a fatherly rule, yet it
is judgmental. The recognition of human *agency* in history must
take with it the subjection of all such agencies to divine rule
and judgment. The claim that Divine providence is active in
setting nations free and restoring human dignity needs therefore
to be accompanied by the recognition that God is no respecter
of persons, that he disposes power in accordance with his
gracious sovereign will, and that whoever holds power needs to
subject it to God's rule and judgment.

It is difficult to know which powers are "ordained" of God.
What is certain is that "Every man's work shall be made manifest:
for the day shall declare it, because it shall be revealed by fire;
and the fire shall try every man's work of what sort it is. If any
man's work abide which he has built thereupon, he shall receive
a reward. If any man's work shall be burned, he shall suffer loss;
but he himself shall be saved; yet so as by fire". (1 Cor. 3.13–15).

Once we recognize that God is the Lord of history and that
he who said "Behold, I make all things new" is manifestly active
in our generation, we must resist the temptation to claim that the
revolution came to an end with the termination of colonial
rule and the assumption of national sovereignty. As a matter
of fact, although in some places we have seen the end of the
beginning, yet in other places the battle is just begun. The
Christian is called upon under all circumstances to seek and
discern the area of God's immediate activities and fully to involve
himself as an honoured co-worker with God in his creative and
redemptive rule among the nations. This is what determines the
place of Christians and of the Church in the practical details of
nation-building.

Believing in the depravity of man, of course, the Christian
cannot give himself to the idea that the African is always right,
or will always be right. Man as man has it in him under particular
circumstances of pride, self-conceit, greed, over-weening in-
ordinate ambition, etc., to misdirect his efforts in wrong directions
towards the production of evil. The Church will therefore constantly have to warn the societies and especially the political
leaders against these tendencies and other moral perversities
which as history has shown us, have been the downfall of
nations and led to the disappearance of civilizations.

3

THE "WRATH OF GOD" AND THE
THAI THEOLOGIA GLORIAE

KOSUKE KOYAMA

I

PROBLEM:
THE WRATH OF GOD OBSCURED BY
THE *APATHEIA* IDEAL

Lactantius, the Christian apologist active in the early fourth century, wrote a treatise called *De ira Dei*. In this remarkable book he attacked the Epicureans and the Stoics who held the view that God is *without passion* (*apatheia*) and cannot be moved to wrath. Lactantius insisted that *God can be moved to wrath*. He said that God is righteous and acts juridically, rewarding the good and punishing the evil. God's wrath is the act by which God punishes wrong doers. Here Lactantius rendered a great apologetic contribution in distinguishing the image of the biblical God from the predominant philosophico-religious piety of his day. The God of the Bible is not the *summum bonum*, the tranquil absolute *apatheia*. It is possible for God to have wrath, the radically perturbed mind (*perturbationes animi*). The righteous God is *perturbed* by the unrighteousness of man.

This insight of Lactantius, voiced against the ancient Stoic ideal of life, needs to be spoken once again against the popular Christian piety in Thailand today. Prevalent religious sentiment in Thailand, including that of Christians, is unwittingly under the influence of the doctrine that *perturbationes animi* are an obnoxious hindrance to the realization of the higher quality of religious life. The call to *apatheia* is not a monopoly of Stoicism. It had been issued by the Gautama Buddha before the time of Stoicism and is a cardinal teaching of Thai Theravada Buddhism. The biblical message of the wrath of God is, as it was to the Stoics, a stumbling-block to the spiritual and intellectual climate of this "Asokan" Stoic country. *Perturbationes animi* are to be eschewed. So the Christian doctrine of the wrath of God, the divine *perturbationes animi*, has been soft-pedalled or avoided.

When the wrath of God was branded as *perturbationes animi* and ignored, some vital message, specifically for Thailand, contained in the doctrine of the wrath of God was lost. What is that message?

In his work, *The Theology of the Pain of God*, Kazo Kitamori, the Japanese theologian, has contributed the penetrating insight that the love of God is distorted and made superficial when it is divorced from the wrath of God. Kitamori's warning that the wrath of God precludes an easy "love monism" sheds light upon the Thai theological situation today. It is true that "love monism" is widely preached in the Thai Church. But Kitamori's insight into the sickness of "love monism", though an extremely important one, cannot be directly applied to the problem in which we are involved in Thailand.

Luther, the giant proponent of the theology of "Triumph of Grace", restored the critical reality of the wrath of God to Christian life and theology. The wrath of God reinterpreted by Luther (for instance, *opus alienum dei* or man's agonizing experience of *opus alienum dei*, i.e., "Anfechtung") by refusing to come under the control of the natural *intellectus* of Aristotelianism, shook the foundation of the "Scholastic Captivity of God". This great Reformational discernment that the wrath of God contradicts man's domestication of God supplies us with a helpful hint for the examination of the Thai theological situation.

The Thai mind tends to identify God with an absolutistic idea beyond history (timeless "apathetic" God). But the wrath of God has an unique power to "historicize" God. In short, if God can truly be moved to wrath, he cannot be a timeless "apathetic" God beyond history, but he must be "God in history" ("Thou" in history), in the sense of the drama described in the Bible. The "God in history" who can be meaningfully moved to wrath cannot be domesticated. The God who is severed from history cannot be meaningfully moved to wrath but can be domesticated. The "wrath of God" is the critical expression of "God in history". This is the message which was thrown out from the Thai Christian life with the despised *perturbationes animi*.

It is the contention of the writer that Thai theology, bolstered by an indigenous *apatheia* ideal, tends inadvertently to neglect

"God in history" by reducing the wrath of God to a matter of minor significance.

II

TWO *LEIMOTIFS* OF
THAI *APATHEIA* RESPONSIBLE FOR
"NEGLECT OF HISTORY"

More specifically, how is it that when the wrath of God is underrated by the *apatheia* ideal, the sense of history also loses seriousness? To deal with this question we must examine the structure of Thai *apatheia*.

The Thai version of the *apatheia* derives from, at least, two dominant sources: 1. influence from Buddhism, and 2. influence from Nature.

1. Influence from Buddhism:
According to *Udana*,[1] as in any other document of Pali Buddhism, the life of spiritual imperturbability (*passaddhi, santi*) is the ideal for every monk. "The one who has crossed over (the swamp of desire)", *Udana* reads, "crushed down the thorn of lust, and destroyed delusion, will not tremble again (if touched) by joy or pain". (22) "The monk who has subdued the thorn of lust, remains unmoved like a mountain peak (in a storm) by insult, punishment, and imprisonment". (23) These passages indicate an *apatheia* piety similar to that of the Stoic Wise. But Buddhism and Stoicism differ decisively in the way in which this envied state of the imperturbable soul is to be reached.

Udana urges man, if he wants to possess the sacred land of imperturbability of soul, to *step out* of all *karmic* chains once for all. So far as man is bound by the inexorable law of causality, that is to say, so far as man is within time and existence (history), he is inevitably and inescapably bound by the power of perturbation. The 30th Word of *Udana* reads: "Mankind is attached to existence, is afflicted with existence, and even more-over rejoices in existence. Of what one rejoices in, that leads to fear. Of what one is afraid, that is miserable. Indeed one leads this holy life in order to escape completely from existence. . . . Truly, this suffering arises in dependence on (karmatic) accumulations. If all attachment (by means of wisdom) is destroyed, (no further) suffering grows up. . . . The complete destruction of thirst and the complete cessation of lust mean the realisation of extinguishment (i.e., Nibbana)". This final *stepping out* of all which is historical is accomplished by the realization of the radical "No-self" (*anatta*). *Anatta* is the perfect state of *apatheia*. How, indeed, can "No-Self" be perturbed?

The Buddhist *apatheia* which is based on the doctrine of *anatta* goes one decisive step further than that of Stoicism. Stoicism teaches man to keep "the six sense spheres of contact under control" (*Udana* 25), but it does not teach to forsake "the organizing forces of existences" (*Udana* 51). The Stoic doctrine of *apatheia* is guided by the same principle which governs the cosmos, namely, that the rule of *logos* (*ratio*) within man leads him to the impertubable life. An inner "orderliness" is the state free from *perturbationes animi*. *Udana* advocates the ultimate annulment of order itself by *stepping out* of it once for all, which amounts to *anatta*. Buddhism promises the transcendental metaphysical solution while Stoicism offers a psychological immanental solution. The former finds the final solution *outside* of history (*logos* and time), the latter, *within* history (*logos* and time). This difference may illustrate one of the most critical points of difference between the Buddhist (anti-historical) East and Christian ("God in history") West. Generally speaking, Christianity, which proclaims the Incarnate Logos, can go with the Stoic ethos but it finds difficulty in getting along with the "will to devaluate history" of Buddhism.

The Buddhist *apatheia* fosters "neglect of history" because it teaches that only through the ultimate flight from history (*anatta*) can man achieve the desired state of *apatheia*.

2. *Influence from Nature:*
How does nature influence the Thai mind towards the "neglect of history"?

From time immemorial nature has impressed man with the view that the flow of time is cyclical. This is nature's interpretation of "history" which is human and universal. Bishop Newbigin writes:

> The dominant patterns of our own experience are cyclical, not linear. The cycles of days and weeks and years, of vegetable and animal life, of human birth, growth, old age and death, all naturally suggest an interpretation of history in cyclical terms. Indeed human institutions and civilizations apparently go through the same cycle of birth, growth, decay, and death.[2]

The cyclical flow of time is strongly felt in agrarian Thailand where the people live in close contact with nature. There are cyclical "biocosmic rhythms"[3] which govern Thai spiritual and cultural life. In Thailand, benevolent nature circles without disruption *ad infinitum* with a cosmic regularity. Thailand has scarcely experienced tidal waves, volcanic eruptions, earthquakes, tornadoes, storms, severe cold, drought or avalanches. Nature is not "perturbed". It is seldom moved to wrath. Time walks on the "road from Jerusalem to Jericho" without encountering serious moments of crisis or decision. Nature, in Thailand, is an efficient teacher of "optimism" of life.[4] It allows man to live a crisis-free mode of life. Even when a crisis occurs, nature persuades man not to be disturbed. Thus the benevolent nature of Thailand has an anti-historical intent. That is to say, nature, represented in the image of a perpetual flow of time in a circle, neglects history, the "road from Jerusalem to Jericho", where the kind of situations which cause *perturbationes animi* are certain to arise. In spite of critical political changes, the advent of giant technology, and rapid westernization of metropolitan suburban life. The Thai mind is basically more "cosmos oriented" than "history oriented". The "cosmos oriented" man does not grasp the seriousness of crises. Crises, when interpreted in the framework of nature's cyclical time, lose their seriousness. "Cyclical time" is the image of *apatheia* translated into the language of time.

Nature influences man to the "neglect of history" because the sense of history is too serious for her and it disrupts her essential message that "all is cyclical and reversible, therefore do not be perturbed! Stay on the side of *apatheia*".

These two dominant sources of the Thai *apatheia*, the desire for the ultimate flight from history to the realm of *anatta*, and the inclination towards undisrupted cyclical outlook of life, join hands in inducing man to adopt a habit of thought which *neglects history*.

III

THE WRATH OF GOD
AND THE THEOLOGY OF
"NEGLECT OF HISTORY"
THEOLOGIA GLORIAE

Theology of "neglect of history" is the theology of God who *stepped out* of history (God of oriental deism) and who therefore cannot be meaningfully moved to wrath. It is also the theology of God who is held captive in the "continual" cyclical flow of cosmic time (God of Nature's Pelagianism) and cannot be meaningfully moved to wrath. It is obvious that theological thinking cannot be put into crisis by the God of oriental deism and nature's Pelagianism. Thus the theology of the "neglect of history" is basically an unperturbed theology. It expresses the essential character of the Thai *theologia gloriae*.

The theology of "neglect of history" at work can be demonstrated by three distinct points in theological thinking.

First, the theology of "neglect of history" is not fully aware of the problems relating to "Revelation and Reason". The perennial headache of Western theology, the tension between revelation and reason, is scarcely a trouble in a culture where the will to devaluate history rules, consciously or unconsciously, through the *apatheia* ideal. How can one be disturbed by the problem of revelation and reason when history, the *locus* of revelation and reason, is under the pressure of the anti-history forces of *"anatta"* and "cyclical" piety, and is thus deprived of its seriousness? Theology of the "neglect of history" is a "stratospheric flight" over the mountains of revelation and reason to a final answer! It wants to be "enlightened" without being entangled in history, the *locus* of revelation and reason. In this sense, the Thai theology of "neglect of history" is *fides otiosa*, a lazy faith.

Second, the theology of "neglect of history" is little capable of perceiving the deep existential meaning of the "strange work of God" (*opus alienum dei*—Isa. 28.21), Christian life and theology. Christian faith is, in its depth, inevitably confronted by the tormenting question of the "strange work of God". The "strange work of God" is neither super-historical nor super-natural work but the work which is experienced *within history*, as the forsaking of Christ by God took place in the historical crucifixion. When the "strange work of God" is approached by the mind of "anti-history flight" and "cyclical continuity" it loses its grave significance.

The theology of "neglect of history" does not want to give serious consideration to history as the *locus* of the *overcoming* of "Anfechtung". Quickly passing over the "strange work of God" it comes to the God of "proper work" (*opus proprium*). In this speedy transition, the moralism dominant in Thai Christian life finds its encouraging support. God who is severed from the critical sense of the "strange work of God" is the reasonable God of moralism characterized by the motif of continuity. In fact, however, God without "strange work" is, as Luther tirelessly testifies, God without "proper work". The theology of "neglect of history" dissolves the existential tension between the "strange work" and "proper work" of God and at the same time makes God understandable to man. It teaches an oriental version of *Christianity not Mysterious*.

Third, the theology of "neglect of history" fails to see the "qualitative difference" between God and man. How can one come to know this crucial "difference" if he is not consciously involved in history, the *locus* of the particular encounter which takes place between "I and Thou"? This fault is reflected in the use of analogy in Thai theological thinking. In the theology of "neglect of history", the analogy works in the framework of circular continuity. That is to say, there is no disruption between finite and infinite. Man must resort to analogy when he speaks of God, but in doing so he is confronted by the God who constantly perturbs his use of analogy. This paradoxial burden in theological thinking is not sufficiently understood by the theology of "neglect of history".

The above three observations exemplify the theology "neglect of history" in operation. The contention of this study is that the wrath of God (not a "timeless" doctrine of the wrath of God) attacks the root of this theology of "neglect of history" which sprang chiefly from the two sources of the dislike of *perturbationes animi*. How is this attack possible? How can the wrath of God "historicize" God in the midst of the subtle influence of the "apathetic" *theologia gloriae* characterized, for instance, by "stratospheric flight", *"Christianity not Mysterious"* and "God who is continuous with man"? But why the wrath of God? Does not the love of God also "historicize" God and stand as a charge against the theology of "neglect of history"? And perhaps more creatively?

The answer is that in Thailand where the Gospel of Christ is encircled by the spirit of *theologia gloriae*, of *non perturbationes animi*, it requires the openly contradicting force of God's *perturbationes animi*, the wrath of God, in order to break through the front line of the anti-historical *theologia gloriae*. The love of God, very often lost in "love monism" ("cheap love"), lacks the *disturbing and critical imagery* which the wrath of God carries. It also lacks the impact which is needed to awaken the mind captivated by the theology of "neglect of history".

A head-on collision between Thai *theologia gloriae* and the wrath of God presents opportunity for a fresh and more relevant study of the doctrine of the wrath of God. Granted that there is a danger of falling into naive anthropopathism, it is essential to preach on the wrath of God boldly to the Thai audience, specifically in order to "historicize" God in the way the Bible does.

According to Dahlberg, the wrath of God is "the Deity's threatening with annihilation the existence of whatever opposes his will and purpose or violates his holiness and love".[5]

It must be made clear that the wrath of God is provoked by the *historical* violation of God's "holiness and love" as for example:

> Remember and do not forget how you provoked the Lord your God to wrath in the wilderness; from the day you came out of the land of Egypt, until you came to this place, you have been rebellious against the Lord. (Deut. 9.7).

The biblical passages of the divine *perturbationes animi* must be read with the insight that the God who *stepped out* of history or the God who is captive to *cyclical* motion cannot be meaningfully moved to wrath. To quote only a few out of innumerable places referring to the wrath of God, such as:

> They have stirred me to jealousy with what is no god;
> they have provoked me with their idols.
> So I will stir them to jealousy with those who are no people;
> I will provoke them with a foolish nation. (Deut. 32.21)

> Ah, Assyria, the rod of my anger,
> the staff of my fury!
> Against a godless nation I send him,
> and against the people of my wrath
> I command him,
> to take spoil and seize plunder,
> and to tread them down like the mire
> of the streets. (Isaiah 10:5.6).

> You only have I known
> of all the families of the earth;
> therefore I will punish you
> for all your iniquities. (Amos 3.2.).

These passages speak emphatically of the fact that God's wrath has *historical* and *covenantal* reasons. That is to say, history is

D

the *locus* of God's *perturbationes animi*. God can be the *summum bonum*, the tranquil *apatheia* if he is not involved in "Heils-geschichte" (History of Salvation—Covenant). This "God in history" perturbs the theology of "neglect of history" with its three distinctive offsprings, "stratospheric flight", *"Christianity not Mysterious"*, and "God who is continuous with man". It does so by making history seriously *real*. The "stratospheric flight" is grounded because history has forced it to realize the vanity and irresponsibility of such flight over revelation and reason. Christianity becomes "mysterious" once more by the historical interpretation of the "strange work of God" and God is no more continuous with man because of the unique quality of encounter which takes place in history between "I and Thou".

CONCLUSION

The wrath of God contradicts the theology of "neglect of history", the theology under the unfluence of the Thai *apatheia* ideal (the *"anatta*-istic" flight from history and the naturalistic aversion for the seriousness in history) by insisting upon the fundamental relationship between the wrath of God and history. *God can be moved to wrath because he is "God in history"*: or, only "God in history" can be meaningfully moved to wrath.

The breaking through of the front line of the "apathetic" *theologia gloriae* made by the assertion of the historicity of the wrath of God needs to be deepened and substantiated by the "sense of the presence of God" who came into history in person, Christ, the *deus incarnatus* who was not *Christos apathes*.

4

SOME AFRICAN CONCEPTS
OF CHRISTOLOGY[1]

JOHN S. MBITI

The title of this paper is misleading because African concepts of Christology do not exist. About 25–30% of African people are Christian. The Church exists in our continent, she is growing and continues to exert great influence upon the life of our peoples. But it is a Church without a theology, without theologians, and without theological concern. My comments do not refer to the ancient Church in Egypt and Ethiopia in which the picture is certainly different. Missionaries who, with the help of African converts, established the Church in the rest of the continent, were not practising theologians, even though they were devout, sincere, and dedicated men and women. This is the state of affairs that we have inherited: current missionaries are not theologians, and the few who claim to be theologians have not yet made much academic contribution; our pastors have little education, and only a few have studied at universities. In the whole of Africa there are (in 1967) not more than about half-a-dozen to ten African theologians engaged in active theological activities. It is in vain therefore, that we try to search for theological reflection from the Church in Africa, at present.

But theological reflection must be started. The task will have to take into account four rich sources of material. These are: the Bible, the theology of the older Churches, the traditional African concepts, and the living experience of the Church in Africa. These are the four pillars on which theological systems of the Church in Africa could be erected. The Bible is the Church's book and the final authority on religious matters. The older Churches, especially in Europe, have a rich inheritance of theological thought, scholarship, tradition, *instrumenta studiorum*, all of which we must utilize, since these are the resources that the Church through the ages has gathered and produced. It would be a sheer waste of time and energy if African theologians began to trace the paths of scholarship already so thoroughly trodden and explored by eminent thinkers of the older Churches.

The third pillar is the traditional African world, with its cultures and histories, its fears and joys, its concerns and worries, its weakness and strength, its inheritance and potentialities. This cannot be ignored: on the contrary, it must be taken seriously. It is within the traditional thought-forms and religious concerns that our peoples live and try to assimilate Christian teaching. These traditional thought-forms strongly colour much of their understanding of the Christian Message. Similar processes have taken place in every society where the Christian Faith has been presented.

Fourthly, the source of material for our theological reflection is the living experience of the Church, what one might call "Practical Theology". This pertains to the Church as she makes her presence felt, as she expands numerically and deepens spiritually, as she carries forth her witness and as she ministers to the needs of the people in every field of their life.

These are sources no doubt provide much material which presents the great difficulty of trying to harmonize and co-ordinate it into a meaningful whole. This is one of the duties facing African theologians, and it is in the performing of this stupendous task, that we will probably be making our contribution to the theology of the universal Church.

With these introductory comments we may now turn to the subject of African Concepts of Christology. Textual, critical, and historical problems of New Testament Christology are well presented in the standard works on the subject.[2] It is unnecessary in a short article like this, to try to summarize these works, or to trace the ground so thoroughly covered. I want to raise only two main problems here. The first is to ask what Christological points have special or strong interest among African Christians, why and how they grasp these points. The second is to ask how the Person of Jesus Christ fits into African conceptualization of the world, and what points of contact the New Testament portrait of Jesus establishes with the African traditional concepts.

CHRISTOLOGICAL POINTS
OF INTEREST TO AFRICAN CHRISTIANS

A short scientific study of sermon texts used by one leading independent Church[3] in West Africa has been made by Harold W. Turner, published under the title *Profile through Preaching*, London, (1965). With regard to sermon materials, this study indicates the type of passages and scripture themes used in this Church which are not under the control or direct influence of missionaries or older Churches. One of the reasons for these sects established and run by Africans, is a search for freedom of expressing the Faith in a manner suitable to African conditions and background, which has not always been achieved in denominations under the control of missionaries from Europe and America.[3] Dr Turner's study makes it possible for us to begin to see something of the points of interest in, at least, one group of African Christians, whether it is representative of the whole or not.

According to this study, of the four Gospels, St Matthew's is the most popular, followed by that of St John, then St Luke and finally St Mark. On the teaching of Jesus, the Sermon on the Mount is the most popular in St Matthew's Gospel, and there is no interest in his arguments about the fulfilment of Old Testament Scriptures. In St John's Gospel, interest is focussed on the story of Nicodemus, teaching about the Holy Spirit, and about Love as the new commandment. In St Luke's Gospel much interest is shown in the parables peculiar to this Gospel. In St Mark's, there is little interest except on the teaching about praying, receiving, and watching.

Concerning the life of Jesus in the four Gospels, there is interest and emphasis on the Triumphal Entry into Jerusalem (in Matthew's Gospel); on the Resurrection (in John's Gospel); the infancy stories, the temptation account, and Jesus' victory over the devil through the Holy Spirit and fasting (in Luke's Gospel); and on the Crucifixion and Resurrection (in Mark's Gospel).

Regarding the practical works of Jesus great emphasis is laid on the miracles of healing, miracles of deliverance, blessing, and judgment.

Of the Pauline epistles, Ephesians is the most popular, followed by Galatians, Romans, I Corinthians, Colossians, and Philippians. Christological interest in these epistles includes emphasis on the

Ressurection passage in I Cor. 15. 12–58 and on the great passage of Christ's exhalation in Philippians 2. 9–11.

This independent Church group puts emphasis on Christian endurance and trust in I Peter, but shows no special interest in Christ's sufferings (3. 18–22) as such. In Hebrews, great emphasis is upon Christ as the High Priest (4.14—5.10), Faith (11), the fate of falling away (10. 19-39), the Promise of the new Rest (3.7—4.13), the Old and New Covenants, and finally Christ's Passion. There is lack of interest in Christ's death and sacrifice as such.

From the book of Revelation, this independent Church lays emphasis on the Last Judgment (20.11–15; 21.7–9), the Millennial Kingdom (20.4–10), the New Jerusalem (21.1–6, 10–22.5), and Judgment both in the prologue and epilogue (1; 22.6–21).

We may summarize this survey by saying that, on the life of Jesus, great emphasis is laid on his birth, Triumphal Entry, his death and resurrection. Of these, the dominating interest is in the resurrection of Jesus and of those who are incorporated into him. In other words, Jesus is seen as the *Christus Victor* above all other things. The interest in his entry into Jerusalem points in the same direction, as do also his miracles of healing and deliverance. Why, we may now ask, does *Christus Victor*, seem to have this special appeal to African Christians?

Africa knows all too well that there are many forces and powers at work in the world. These are both real and imaginary, but they include spiritual powers, spirits, witchcraft, sorcery, fear, anxiety, sickness, diseases, the power of evil and the greatest of them all, death. In traditional life, people always find a rational explanation for misfortunes and other manifestations of evil, normally blaming any of the above items as the cause. There are measures taken to protect people from witchcraft, others to exorcise the spirits or keep them away, others to bring success in life, others to heal and cure sickness, and many other measures to counteract as much evil and suffering as possible. Africa has many myths explaining how these evil experiences of human life originated. The chief of these myths tell how men lost God's original gift of immortality, resurrection, and rejuvenation.[4] Man lost these gifts and came to accept his poverty as a *fait accompli*. Traditional African concepts of time are heavily directed towards the past and the present, but with practically no projection in the future direction beyond two years or so. In all its richness of mythology concerning what happened in the past, traditional African societies have no knowledge or mythology of the future.

There is nothing in traditional concepts promising or hoping for a reversal of the experiences described in myths of the past. There is nothing to redeem men from the loss of immortality, resurrection, and rejuvenation. This never dawned on the thinking of our peoples, nor did they ever conceive of a supra-human conqueror of evil among men. It is here that the portrait of Jesus as *Christus victor* comes in and fits in most readily. There exists in traditional concepts a great vacuum in this direction, and Jesus immediately fills up that vacuum, drawing attention first and foremost as the Victor over the forces which have dominated African life from time immemorial. *Christus Victor* at once reminds our peoples of the loss of immortality which he now restores; of the loss of the resurrection, which he now brings about in his own life and in the promise that those in him will be resurrected; and of the loss of rejuvenation, which now in Jesus begins to take place leading towards the eschatological climax when God will make all things new.

The Christian message brings Jesus as the one who fought victoriously against the forces of the devil, spirits, sickness, hatred, fear, and death itself. In each of these areas he won a victory and lives now above the assault of these forces. He is the victor, the one hope, the one example, the one conqueror: and this makes sense to African peoples, it draws their attention, and it is pregnant with meaning. It gives to their myths an absolutely new dimension. The greatest need among African peoples, is to see, to know, and to experience Jesus Christ as the victor over the powers and forces from which Africa knows no means of deliverance. It is for this reason that they show special interest in the Temptation of Jesus and his victory over the devil through the power of the Holy Spirit. They know that the devil is not just an academic problem but a reality, manifesting his power through ways such as unwanted spirit possessions, sickness, madness, discord, fights, murders, and so on.

It is interesting that in the Pauline epistles the "Aladura Church" shows little or no interest in doctrine, except the doctrine of the Resurrection in I Cor. 15, and the doctrine of Christ's exaltation in Philippians 2.9–11. We have said much about *Christus Victor*, let us now draw attention to something else.

The Birth, Baptism, and Death of Jesus are given emphasis

by this Aladura Church, and no doubt by other African
Christians. What do these events mean? Here I would suggest
that the African view of Man may throw light on this problem.
Two relevant comments must here be made. One is that God
creates the child, gives it to the community. Secondly, the
community must now incorporate that child into total human
society. A person must go through a process of incorporation,
generally by means of *rites de passage*, before he can be considered a full human being. Normally there are four (or three)
rites de passage: birth, initiation (at adolescence, generally),
marriage, and finally death. These are the stages through which a
person wins full recognition as a complete, entire member of
society.

The *rites de passage* at birth incorporate the child into the
human society, making it a passive member of the community.
At initiation, he is incorporated into the status of a responsible,
active member of the community, and receives the duties, rights,
privileges, and responsibilities which go with this new status.
Marriage rites make him a reproductive member of the
community, linking him with the dead and those yet to be born,
giving him the torch of life, and making him a nucleus of a
new family. Death rites are acts of separation from the society
of the living, making the dead join the community of the
departed. Yet, paradoxically, the dead are not dead: they are
very close to the living. This fact is externalized in the acts of
libation and offering of food by the living to their departed
relatives as a sign of fellowship, communion, and oneness.

I suggest, that the Birth, Baptism, and Death of Jesus, attract
the special attention of African Christians because they portray
Jesus as a perfect man, the one who has gone through the
necessary *rites de passage*. It is for this reason that African
Christians show interest in the geneological tables in Matt. 1.1–17
and Luke 3.23–38. In Ephesians and Revelation, the Church is
spoken of metaphorically as the Bride or Wife of our Lord. So
in effect, in the eyes of African peoples, for whom these *rites
de passage* are so meaningful, Jesus fulfils everything which
constitutes a complete, corporate member of society. It would
be surprising if African peoples did not show interest in these
key moments of life. It is *not* primarily in the sacrificial interpretation of Christ's death that Africans see the significance of
the cross. The cross is not a sign of shame and humiliation:

but a symbol of completeness as far as the human life of Jesus was concerned. He died on the cross because he was a perfect, complete, entire, mature and responsible Man. He just had to die, and the cross merely happened to be the means by which he died. To emphasize this point is by no means intended to deprive the death of our Lord of its sacrificial and soteriological consequences. These consequences derive from, rather than lead to, the cross: they are the effects rather than the causes of the cross. It was as an ordinary man that Jesus died, and the great Christian *differentia* comes obviously from the fact of the Resurrection by which the Christian faith stands or falls. What happens before Easter is an experience which men share. What happens after Easter is the uniqueness of the gospel, the exception which is to be the norm for all who are incorporated into Christ.

The New Testament is clear on this point—that Jesus died because he was a perfect Man: he had taken unto himself, all that constituted humanity except the experience of sin. Heb. 2.17f. reminds us that "he had to be made like his brethren in every respect. . . . For because he himself has suffered and been tempted, he is able to help those who are tempted". Again in the same chapter 2.14, we hear that "since therefore the children share in flesh and blood, he himself likewise partook of the same nature, that through death he might destroy him who has the power of death. . . .' The same note is struck in Phil. 2.7, that Jesus "emptied himself, taking the form of a servant, being born in the likeness ($\dot{o}\mu o\iota\dot{\omega}\mu\alpha\tau\iota$) of men". Again in Rom. 8.3, Jesus is said to have been sent by God, "in the likeness ($\dot{o}\mu o\iota\dot{\omega}\mu\alpha\tau\iota$) of sinful flesh". These are but a few of the indications from the New Testament that there is no shadow of doubt that Jesus was a full man, without sharing the sinful part of human life. It was as such that he died, thus completing his identification with humanity. The same process working in reverse means that it is now only through our identification with him that we can hope and expect to be made like him in his exaltation.

THE PORTRAIT OF JESUS
IN THE AFRICAN CONCEPTUALIZATION
OF THE WORLD

Here I can only raise question without supplying adequate answers to them. They revolve around the question: What do

African Christians think of the Person of Christ? The New Testament and early Christian literature use various titles to describe or portray Jesus. These titles include the Messiah, the Son of God, the Servant of God, David's Son, the Lord, the Saviour, the Christ, the Son of Man, and several others. We must ask, therefore, whether these titles have any meaning for African believers, and if so, what?

One must here safeguard against the danger of taking a nationalistic view of Jesus, thus reducing him to fit into a national image, whether Greek, German, African, or Asian. This mistake has been made repeatedly in the course of Church history and at times with disastrous consequences. But there are thought-forms, concepts, associations, and cultural backgrounds which affect and influence our understanding whether of simple or complex items.

Of these major titles of Jesus, the Messiah, the Christ, the Son of David, and the Son of Man have no special relevance to traditional African concepts. Some are historically rooted, others are bound up with the Jewish eschatological hope, and there are no parallels in African thought-forms, histories, and traditions. As such it is difficult to understand them, let alone to recognize their christological significance. African Christians show little, if any, interest in the picture of Jesus conjured up by this group of titles, because it is hard, if not impossible, to convey intelligibly to them the meaning of them. This group does not fit into the thought-forms of African peoples, and has no real influence on their understanding of Christ. This does not mean, however, that the titles are rejected: they are simply dormant, like buds in the winter.

The other group of titles has relevance to the traditional background and can, therefore, mean something. These are titles such as the Son of God, Lord, the Servant of God, and possibly Saviour or Redeemer. Let us look at these titles and see what they may convey to African peoples.

The concept of the Son of God is not altogether foreign to them. That there can be this Father-Son relationship in the Godhead does not seem impossible to a number of African peoples. The Ndebele and Shona of Rhodesia conceive of God in a trinitarian context of Father, Son, and Mother. The Shilluk of the Sudan refer to their king as the "first-born of God", "child of God", "last-born of God", etc. The Dogon of Upper Volta visualize God as having an aspect known as *Nommo* and defined as "the Son of God ... the appointed model of creation".[5] A number of examples can be quoted from African mythology in which God is represented as having a Son, e.g. the Bemba of Zambia call their national founder "the Son of God". The Sonjo of Tanzania believe that their national and religious hero simply appeared without mother or father, that he died, rose again, ascended to God (or the sun) and is now identified with God.[6] We must not suggest in the least that any of these traditional concepts of sons of God should be regarded as on an equal footing with the title and position of Jesus as the Son of God. The point here is that the ground is fertile in which to plant this christological title. These traditional figures and concepts are an aid to grasping and understanding Jesus as the Son of God. Similarly, the obedience of the Son to the Father, as portrayed in the life of Jesus, fits without difficulty into our traditional concepts of father-son relationship in the home. We could pursue this point further, and examine, *inter alia*, Jesus' use of the term "Father" and especially of the christologically pregnant word "Abba" which has been transmitted into the New Testament in more or less its original Aramaic form.[7]

It is not difficult to make contact with traditional thought-forms, in considering the title of Lord ($\kappa\acute{\nu}\rho\iota\sigma$) as applied to Jesus. Some of our peoples refer to God as Lord, or Master. The immediate background here is naturally the political set up, especially in societies which had traditional rulers (like chiefs and kings). This is not in the least to suggest that the septuagint Kurios, which is transposed in the New Testament and applied to Jesus, is to be regarded as being parallel to these traditional concepts of "the Lord", But the opportunity is there for the basis on which contact could be established. After all, the septuagint Kurios has also among other meanings its political undertones,[8] and especially in the time of the Roman emperors, during whose rule the Church and the New Testament came into being. Our point here is to emphasize that the Lordship of Jesus can be fitted into the African concept of his person and position. He would indeed shine through as the Lord of lords, since Africa knows also of other lords besides God.

The Servant of the Lord is another title which can be fitted into the African concept of Jesus. Among some of our peoples, it is believed that God has servants who are obedient to him, whom he sends with his message to the world, some of whom took part in the creation of the world or in early human history. Thus for example, in Fon (of Dahomey) cosmology there is a being (Da) who, during creation, acted as God's assistant and organizer of the world.[9] The Tiv of Nigeria believe that God has an assistant who reminds him when it is time to give men rain. The Chagga of Tanzania tell that God had a messenger or servant whom he sent to warn people of the consequences of their wickedness, but when men did not forsake their evil ways God sent this servant and destroyed nearly all the people. The Vugusu of Kenya say that God has servants who are the spirits of men who died long ago. Our point here is that the portrait of Jesus as the servant of the Lord establishes contact with traditional concepts, and it is easy to present it meaningfully to our peoples.

In traditional African concepts, there are no parallels with the title of "the Saviour". Our myths look back to the creation of the world, the early men, the coming of death into the world, the separation between God and men, heaven and earth. There is nothing that looks towards the future, nothing to be awaited and nothing to be expected in the future apart from the rhythm of day and night, birth, initiation, marriage, death and entry into the company of the departed. But, precisely because of this obvious gap with regard to matters of life, death, resurrection, and reconciliation with God, the concept of Jesus as Saviour strikes the African world with dynamic meaning. This portrait of Jesus fits into the yearning and longing of our peoples fulfilling something for which there has been no other known means of fulfilment. It is as if they awaited in darkness, not knowing that a Saviour would come. For generations African peoples have handed down by word of mouth myths of how paradise was lost, how immortality was lost, how death came about, how God and men were separated, and so on, but nobody knew how this loss could be repaired, how the resurrection could be regained, how the gap between God and men could be bridged. But in Jesus all this falls into place; it makes sense, it becomes a revelation, a hope, and a destiny to which the Church and the Heilsgeschichte are moving. It is for this reason, perhaps, that the independent Church to which we referred in the first part of this essay takes great interest in the new Jerusalem, in the portrait of Jesus as the *Christus*

Victor, and in his works of healing the sick, exorcising the possessed, and delivering the captives.

Jesus as the Redeemer opens the way and possibility for men to be reconciled and to become akin to God. Because, in the African image of man, Jesus is seen as a perfect, complete man; and because he is seen as the Son of God, he is entitled to mediate between God and men. Many of our peoples know the need of mediators between God and men, and some provide them in the persons of priests, spirits, or the departed. That we as men can become akin to God, touches upon a key concept in African traditional life. The concept of kinship dominates almost every aspect of traditional life. Kinship knits together every member of the community. It works vertically, uniting the departed with the living and those yet to be born. It works horizontally, uniting every individual with every other individual so that within a village or neighbourhood every person is a relative of every other person. Consequently each person has one "biological" father but a hundred kinship fathers; one biological mother, but a hundred kinship mothers; perhaps three biological brothers, but a hundred kinship brothers; and similarly hundreds of sisters, cousins, grandmothers, and so on. Likewise every person is father, mother, sister, brother, etc. towards everybody else in the network of kinship. This is the structure of the traditional solidarity based and grounded upon kinship through blood and marriage. The individual says: "I am because we are and, since we are, therefore I am". He is conscious of himself only in terms of the corporate group. This is the context within which the individual discovers himself in the traditional tribal solidarity of African communities.

The question now is, can the Church, as the Body of Christ, take over this consciousness of self-existence, transposing the individual from the tribal solidarity to the Christian or Church solidarity centred and rooted in Jesus Christ? This I believe is possible, but it has hardly begun to take place in the Church in Africa. The New Testament lays great emphasis on the concept of corporate existence in Christ. St Paul's constant use of the metaphor of "the Body" ($\tau\grave{o}$ $\sigma\hat{\omega}\mu\alpha$) to refer to the Church is the key concept in his entire theology. The new man in Christ is referred to corporately as "the Body of Christ", the Church, of which individuals are its corporate members. The African field is ripe for this contact to be established, and for the transposition of tribal solidarity into Christ's solidarity. In Christ, through the new relationship or kinship which he makes possible, the individual discovers his true individuality and simultaneously loses his individualism in order to gain the new corporateness without which he cannot exist. He discovers his existence in two dimensions. First, ἐν Χριστῷ, the individual says: "I am, because Christ is". Secondly he says: "I exist because the Body of Christ exists". At the individual level this is what the new kinship in Christ should mean: a discovery of one's true being as hidden in the Man *par excellence*, and a discovery of one's existence as externalized in the Body of Christ. This is a field of great potentiality in the practical existence of the Church in Africa. It may be that it is here that she will make a great contribution in discovering and experiencing the meaning of kinship in Christ.

Yet it is only within the sacramental life of the Church that this discovery can be made and experienced. Only then can the Church move outwards to exert her influence and make her impact felt in other areas of Church life. It is to be noted that African Christians regard the sacrament of Baptism as being extremely important, and in some sects individuals get baptized as often as ten times or more. The Eucharist on the other hand is given a minor place, or ignored completely, in many congregations. Yet, the Eucharist is pregnant with both eschatological and christological meaning. If the Gospel is to make sense to African peoples it can happen only through their picture and experience of Jesus. It is only by understanding who he is, by experiencing who he is, and by participating in him as he is, that they will be transposed from traditional solidarity, or any other solidarity, to the solidarity of Christ. Could it be that the process of evangelization in Africa has missed the main road by failing to put the Eucharist at the centre of Christian life? Can the Church in any country, in any place and at any time, become aware of herself as the Body of Christ, and get a balanced picture of her Lord, Master, and Nourisher, without placing the teaching and observance of the Sacraments at the centre of her life? Is it not at Baptism and the Eucharist that, *inter alia*, the Christian enters the christological stream, and realizes that "I am because Christ is—both individually and corporately"? These are not just rhetorical questions, but with them we must end this paper.

5

THE ROLE OF CHRISTOLOGY
IN THE CHRISTIAN ENCOUNTER
WITH EASTERN RELIGIONS

CHOAN-SENG SONG

The history of Christian thought is the history of how Christian theologians attempt to give an account of the truth of their faith in the language and thought-forms of their time. This attempt is necessitated both internally and externally: internally because the meaning of the Christian faith and its implications for the Christian life have to be clarified within the fold of the community of believers; externally because there are always people outside the Church challenging the truthfulness of the Christian faith and demanding explanations for its claim of uniqueness. In the course of the development of Christian thought, therefore, many issues and problems have been brought up to be debated and discussed, issues and problems concerning the existence and nature of God, the person and work of Jesus Christ, the raison d'être of the Church, the indicative and imperative of the Christian life, and so on. Though some issues will demand greater attention than others in different periods of time, yet it is true to say that when one particular issue is brought into the centre of the search light of questions and answers other issues are also bound to be re-examined, since "strictly speaking, in Dogmatics and in Church preaching every single statement is at once the basis and the content of all the rest."[1]

This being the case, it is important to observe that theological controversy tends to narrow the scope of its subject-matter and come to be focused, in the long run, on a most vital issue, namely, the Christological issue. In view of this, one can say that the history of Christian thought begins with, is held in tension all the way through by, and will be rejuvenated by the

Christological problem. Even a casual knowledge of creeds and confessions of faith will make us aware of what is at stake in Christian response to God's act in history. In our own time the Christological Confession of the World Council of Churches in Amsterdam in which "The World Council of Churches" is stated to be "composed of Churches which acknowledge Jesus Christ as God and Saviour" becomes a real theological issue for Christians of different shades and creeds.[2] Be that as it may, this state of the matter is anything but strange to the Christian faith. For in a very real sense Jesus Christ himself foresaw this. At the critical turning point in his missionary career Jesus Christ put an astonishing question to his disciples on the solitary road of Caesarea Philippi: "Who do you say that I am?" (Mk. 8.29) It is of utmost significance that it is Jesus Christ himself who raised the Christological question for the first time in dead seriousness. Was the question an expression of his uncertainty about his own person and mission lurking somewhere in his consciousness? Was the meaning of his person and work somehow dependent upon the opinion of others about him? Or was it a form of expressing his self-assurance about his earthly existence deep-rooted always in his mind? We could almost go on asking questions like these endlessly and still find ourselves no nearer a definitive answer. But the situation changes when we realize how the Christological question put by Jesus Christ himself drew out an equally startling answer from Peter who exclaims: "You are the Christ." (Mk. 8.29).

No doubt this was the correct answer. The whole point that this event which took place in Jesus' confrontation with his disciples seems to teach us is that we cannot hope to grasp the meaning of the Being and Act of Jesus Christ by going behind his back or going beyond him. In other words it is the plain truth that Jesus Christ himself is the primary datum of our Christological confession. Where he is present as the suffering Messiah there the Christological question is raised with all seriousness. To put it differently, the Christological question is a real question when it is put to us by Jesus Christ himself through his words or through his mere presence. The Four Gospels can, thus, be regarded as accounts of the Christological dialogues which took place between Jesus Christ and his contemporaries. The crib in humble stable with which his life on earth begins and the Cross on the horrible Golgotha with which it terminates, are they not powerful expressions demonstrating to the whole world in silent eloquence the *terminus a quo* and the *terminus ad quem* of the

Christological problem? When we are confronted by the concrete embodiment of the incarnate Love, are we not already involved in the Christological problem willy-nilly like these two disciples on the Emmaus road whose hearts burnt within them even though they did not realize that they were in the company of the risen Lord (Lk. 24)? It is, therefore, correct to say that it is we who are put into question by the Christological problem and not Jesus Christ. Properly speaking, that is to say Christologically speaking, a Christological question raised from the human side in abstraction from the Being and Act of Jesus Christ is bound to miss the target and thus lapse into irrelevancy. It is a question asked in a vacuum. To put it more forcefully, we could play with the Christological problem only in the absence of Jesus Christ, which to all intents and purposes is an impossible feat. Most of the Christological errors committed in the history of Christian thought are the result of trying to do this impossible thing.

This observation has a far reaching bearing upon the Christian encounter with religions of the East, which is taking place more and more openly and persistently. This is all to the good, for as Brunner puts it, redemption accomplished by Jesus Christ is not redemption *from* the world but redemption *of* the world,[3] which by implication includes religions. Religion, whatever else it may be, is primarily search for salvation—salvation in its varied connotations.[4] The universal quest for salvation, or in Tillich's language the longing for a New Being, is the common ground of all religions. By virtue of his religious instinct, man is somehow aware of the fact that he is not at peace with himself, with his fellowmen, with society, and with the whole of nature. Even the great principle of Comprehensive Harmony presupposed in various systems of Chinese philosophy is not something ready at hand, but something to be restored, to be regained. How is man to overcome these broken relationships is the chief concern of all religions. The final state supposed to be reached through over-coming distorted and estranged relationships is consequently described as salvation, a term which naturally covers a multitude of meanings. Paradoxically enough, however, it is this common ground of salvation in which non-Christian religions try to claim universal likeness of all religions that sets Christians to insist on the utter unlikeness and uniqueness of the Christian faith. And it is, furthermore, on this common ground that battles are fought in earnest in the name of religious salvation. I have no intention

of going into all the details of religious battles fought on behalf
of both Christianity and non-Christian religions. This is a subject
in itself which deserves a separate study and treatment. What
I am concerned to point out in this connection is that all
religious problems seem to boil down in the end to one single
focal point, namely, the person and work of the Christian
Saviour Jesus Christ. And it is at this point that many wrong
Christological questions are asked by non-Christians and wrong
answers are given on the part of Christians. The result is that
there are wilful misunderstanding and naive self-righteousness on
both sides. Under such circumstances it is a matter of urgency
for Christian apologetics living and moving and having its being
in the lands of gods many and lords many to direct its thought
ever afresh to the role of Christology in its encounter with non-
Christian religions. As long as Christians still evade this central
question of the Christian faith a real dialogical encounter of
Christianity with non-Christian religions has not yet taken place.
On the contrary, through honest and pains-taking struggle with
the Christological question put to Christians and non-Christians
alike by Jesus Christ Himself this encounter will bear rich and
meaningful fruits both on the theological and on the confessional
level. It is very significant to discover that non-Christian
apologetics seems to have an inkling of what is at stake in all the
religious problems which have arisen out of the present religious
situation. That is why they are now directing various Christological questions back to Christians. We need to see, therefore,
what are the major questions they are asking before proceeding to
show our own position based on the Christian faith.

Let us take Radhakrishnan first who has been one of the most
articulate spokesmen on behalf of the Hindu faith. Concerning
him Dr. Kitagawa correctly says: "It is his conviction that the
essential truth of all religions is the same. For him, religion is not
a creed or code, but an insight into reality; religion is the life of
the inner spirit—or the affirmation of the primacy of spiritual
values. His synthesis, however, is grounded in Vedanta tradition.
He holds that all that is good is implicit in the Upanishads."[5]
From such general religious presuppositions it is no surprise to
hear him say: "Studies in comparative religion reveal to us not
only the bewildering variety of religious beliefs and practices but
also the many points of resemblance between religious systems
which treat themselves as opposed to each other. Some of the
most significant features like incarnation, miracles, and festivals,

are found in common."[6] The problem of resemblance among religions which the erudite Radhakrishnan constantly raises in his prolific writings is by no means a novel one. The subject has been studied both extensively and intensively during recent years by the so-called myth-and-ritual school in Britain and the Uppsala school which have shown us striking resemblances of religious and cultural patterns throughout the ancient Near Eastern countries including Israel. This is in itself a fascinating subject of study, but this is also the area of study in which much damage has been done by those who suffer from lack of the proper sense of theological judgement. For Radhakrishnan, it is obvious that his chief source of interest lies elsewhere than in the field of objective and scientific study of comparative religion and culture. What he is concerned to do is to affirm his conviction that the essential truth or teaching of all religions is practically the same.[7]

If I am allowed to digress a little, I would like to point out the fact that most of the apologetics of religions in the East always try to claim universality for their religious teachings but never attempt to claim universal validity for their religious founders. They therefore apply the same logic to Christianity, recognizing the teachings of Jesus Christ as something they can share and observe, but refusing to acknowledge in this particular Jesus universal validity which sets him over and above the category of man. In accordance with their religious teaching and religious experiences what they have to aspire to is the merging of the particular with the universal. In other words, their religions offer the possibility of every particular, theoretically speaking, becoming the universal. As to the universal becoming the particular, it means nothing but degeneration and lapse into the bondage of the particular. It is therefore absurd to claim universal validity for the person of anyone who is caught in the samsāra of the particulars just like others. This refusal of the particular in Hinduism is the source of its lack of interest in history. Thus Dr Singh, an Indian theologian, rightly says: "The category of uniqueness is tied up with the conception of history, especially where history is taken seriously. Uniqueness, singularity, etc., are appreciated in the context of a historical religion. Hinduism believes in general rules, principles, and truths. It has very little sense of history. It has, therefore, little or no conception of the category of uniqueness."[8] In spite of this fact, we must recognize that there is a profound wisdom in the Hindu pessimism with regard to the tragic existence of the particular. However this same wisdom becomes instrumental in its mistaken view of Jesus Christ. This is nowhere more explicitly expressed than in the following quotation from Radhakrishnan. "The saving knowledge of God is not knowledge of and faith in Jesus, as a historical person portrayed in the Gospels. Christ is not to be equated with the historical Jesus. Christ is the spirit of the Supreme, the Eternal Word. The manifestation of this Word in history is not limited to Jesus. Salvation is mediated through the Eternal Christ, the Word of God which is not to be confused with the historic Jesus."[9]

Apart from the problem of one incarnation or many incarnations implied in this statement it is highly important for us to see that the religious logic of Hinduism regarding the particular and the universal leads Radhakrishnan into saying something which reminds one of the Arian Christology. As we know, Arius arose from the very centre of Christian religion on doctrinal grounds, while Radhakrishnan stands in the midst of his ideal of a "Commonwealth of Religions",[10] trying to relegate Jesus to the rank of the guru and to assign to Christ a place in the congress of deities by splitting the human Jesus from the divine Christ right in the middle.[11] It also looks like resurrection of the buried corpse of the theological liberalism of the last century which provoked Barthian condemnation and which caused the neo-orthodox theologians to swing their Christological pendulum to the opposite extreme. Radhakrishnan has, however, gone further than both Arius and the liberal theologians of the nineteenth century in having accomplished a double task of relativising both the historical Jesus and the divine Christ. How are we going to deal effectively with this Christology modified by Radhakrishnan in the light of the Hindu faith? How is it possible for us to say that the universal assumed the particular in Jesus Christ in such a way that he is this particuler by virtue of the universal? It is this dichotomy of the particular and the universal in Hindu realism on the one hand and the elevation of the particular in order to be merged and lost in the universal in Hindu mysticism that pose a serious problem for the theologian in the East when he undertakes to reformulate his Christology. It will not do just to assert with Donald T. Rowlingson that Jesus Christ is the "Religious Ultimate."[12] For besides the ambiguity of the term "Religious Ultimate", it is precisely this assumption that has been put into question by Radhakrishnan and others.

It is well for us to remember that Radhakrishnan is not the only Hindu who raises objections against the Christological affirmation of the Nicene-Chalcedonian theology. To give another example, Keshub Chandra Sen, a leading figure in the Brâhmo-Samâj organization, though accepting Jesus Christ as one of the great prophets and the cross as a symbol of self-denial, rejects Christ as the incarnate God. His language is more down to earth than that of Radhakrishnan. He says in effect: " ... Mortal man, with all his frailties ... is deified and worshipped, and to him is rendered that supreme adoration which belongs to God alone! This idolatorous bending of the knee before man is an insult to heaven ... it is a treason against God which pollutes the heart and degrades the soul."[13] Curiously enough here from the lips of a Hindu we hear precisely these words which the scribes heaped upon the head of Jesus Christ: "Why does this man speak thus? It is blasphemy! Who can forgive sins but God alone?" (Mk. 2.7). One of the profoundest ironies in the history of mankind is that when Jesus Christ, the Son of God, has taken upon himself our humanity on account of our salvation, he is constantly rejected as the Saviour of the world on the ground of that very humanity. It may be that as Karl Barth says this is the paradox of God's veiling in his unveiling. Or isn't it possible to say that man rejects the human Jesus because he cannot tolerate himself, his own humanity, in the humanity of Jesus Christ? This seems to be the thought hidden behind those impassioned words of Keshub Chandra Sen. If this is a correct reading of his mind, how close he, a Hindu, is to the biblical view of man! But the tragedy is that in spite of this closeness, or rather because of this closeness, he indignantly moves away from the whole Jesus Christ, who is not only man but also God.

The same is also true of that great human being Gandhi. Perhaps it is not an exaggeration to say that Gandhi's whole life of self-denial and self-sacrifice will put many a devoted Christian to shame and cause them to hide their faces in the sands of remorse. If he had been born and lived in Western Christendom he would have been canonized like St Francis of Assisi or St Benedict of Nursia or many others who adorn the history of the Christian Church. But when we come to think of him in terms of Christology, we cannot help being puzzled by the fact that he showed no interest whatsoever in the person of Jesus Christ. For him what is important is what Jesus has done and not who he is. The concept of the Incarnation was

to him a stumblingblock.[14] In spite of all this Jesus remained
one of the religious powers which shaped and moulded his life
and work.[15] Here we have another example posing us the Christological problem of how the universal could break into history
and dwell in the midst of other particulars without being caught
in the evil net of the samsāra.

With Gandhi we have reached the appropriate point to turn
our attention to the other stream of culture, namely Chinese
culture. The religious air we breathe in Chinese culture is quite
different from that of Indian culture. A pilgrim who travels
from Indian culture to Chinese culture will feel as if he suddenly
becomes aware of himself after having roamed in lands of
mystery semi-consciously. In India religiousness is something
which is taken for granted, whereas in China energetic apologetics
of Chinese culture find it necessary to defend the existence of a
unified religious spirit in the Chinese people. They are the
intellectuals from both rationalist and idealist camps. To deny a
religious spirit to the Chinese is equivalent to denying them their
self-identity as a nation. Therefore even a staunch rationalist
like Hu Shih, in whose eyes religion is nothing more than super-
stition, makes a point of saying that "Chinese philosophy has
always been so much conditioned by the religious development
of the different periods that the history of Chinese thought
cannot be properly understood without being studied together
with that of the Chinese religion."[16] What is then the basic tenet
of religious belief which prevails especially among the intellectuals? It is essentially a religion of man. It has been aptly
summarized as follows: "The ultimate goal of religion, then, is
man's moral perfection. Religion is therefore essentially ethical
and social. . . . We may go a step further and say that to the
Chinese intellectuals the fulfilment of human nature is
religion."[17] The same religious note can be found basically among
the masses, although it tends to appear in a much less refined
form. To quote from the same book again: "Because of their
preoccupation with this world, the religious societies, old and
new, have given very little study to spiritual beings. Their primary
interest has been man and his good life on earth."[18] Thus the
three cardinal happinesses for the common Chinese are: wealth,
children, and long life.

These general characteristics of Chinese indigenous religious
beliefs, regardless of whether they be of the intellectuals or of the
masses, have their eloquent expression in a fascinating book

entitled *From Pagan to Christian* written by Lin Yu-tang. This is a penetrating account of the author's spiritual pilgrimage. He tells us why he became a pagan after having been initiated into theological disciplines and how he found his way back to Christianity again.[19] It was the moral failures on the part of Christians whom he knew to do justice to the Chinese traditional culture that drove him away in fury from the Christian Church. It was again the discovery of the superiority of the ethical teachings of Jesus to other ethical systems that brought him back to the fellowship of the Church. He writes: "Thus it is that the world of Jesus contains both that power, and something else—the absolute clarity of light, without the self-limitation of Confucius, the intellectual analysis of Buddha, or the mysticism of Chuang-tse. Where others reasoned, Jesus taught, and where others taught, Jesus commanded."[20] He rightly observes that it is the spontaneous outflow of love from both Jesus himself and Christians that work miracles in converting people to the God of Jesus Christ. The secret of the power of Christianity, as he conceives it, consists in the fact that Christianity is a religion of action, and not of contemplation. He sums up, then, the essence of Christian theology in the following words: "It seems to me that Christian theology is largely responsible for shifting the emphasis of Christ on 'bearing fruit' and doing his commandments, to some easy-to-take, near-magical formula for salvation which does not require moral effort on the part of the individual and is therefore more palatable."[21]

Perhaps many theologians who have entered the "peaceful" rest will turn uncomfortably in their graves when they hear him say this. But this is not all that he has to say about theology. He goes even further and launches into a wholesale attack on theology, blaming it for being chiefly responsible for his pagan wanderings. "What I am saying", he declares, "is that what prevents men from knowing Jesus is exactly these doctrinaire busybodies; that their confusion of creeds and dogmas kept me from Christianity for thirty years; and that their five-and-ten-cent theology prevented me from seeing Jesus."[22] There is no quarrel over the fact that Jesus Christ of the Gospels and his teachings are central in our inquiries into the nature of the Christian faith. There is also no denying that there have been bad theologies which becloud the light of Jesus Christ. The question, however, is whether or not the Jesus whom Lin Yu-tang sees in the Gospels through his own spectacles is the Jesus the writers of the

Gospels want him to see. He forgets, moreover, the fact that
the picture of Jesus Christ in the New Testament is already a
theological picture. Hence it means that Lin Yu-tang is raising
Christological questions which must be dealt with in theological
terms no matter whether he likes it or not. It will not do for the
Chinese theologian to substitute Christian ethics for Christology in the Chinese Church or in the theological curriculum.
From this theological stand-point we can only take the following
statement with much qualification: "From the unmistakable
ethical emphasis in present-day Chinese religion, it is safe to
predict that the future of religion in China will be deeply this-
wordly and ethical. . . . To grow on Chinese soil, Christianity
must be long on the humanistic and short on the theological
side. One is justified in saying that Chinese development of
Christianity has already followed the ethical tendency."[23] To be
sure, it must be acknowledged that being utterly practical and
pragmatical the Chinese do not seem to have patience with
theological intricacies and complexities which characterize theological controversies down through the centuries in the
history of the Christian Church. But is it not true to say that
because of its failure to come to grips with Christological problems theologically, Christianity, in the eyes of the Chinese, tends
to be regarded as a *mere* ethical religion superior to other ethical
systems only in degree? Granted that in the Gospel stories Jesus
Christ stresses the ethical side of human life. The Sermon on the
Mount will never cease to make radical demands upon the
Christian life. Granted too that in the ethical teachings of Jesus
Christ the Chinese will find access to Jesus Christ. Precisely
because of this, the Chinese theologian cannot escape the
theological task of seeing and helping his countrymen to see
the bearings of Christology upon ethical problems in the right
perspective. In view of this, Francis Wei makes a right observation
when he says: "There are also points of contact between
Christianity and Chinese religious and ethical teachings. To cite
one instance, Chinese culture is fundamentally humanistic. It
does not follow from this that the supernatural elements are
to be slighted in our presentation of the Christian message to the
Chinese. They may need just that which is lacking or weak in
their own culture."[24] Perhaps I should add that it is not just a
matter of the Chinese needing what is lacking or weak in their
own culture, but it is a matter of radical reorientation of their
hearts and minds in the light of a deeper Christological experience

and understanding. The influence of the Christian faith among the Chinese people will grow in depth in proportion to how seriously they take the question put to them by Jesus Christ Himself: "But who do *you* say that I am?"

From what has been described above we have gained some idea of the issues and problems related to Christology as they are conceived and put forth by religious people in the East. Our investigation reveals to us the crucial nature of these issues and problems which contain in themselves both points of contact and points of departure between Christianity and non-Christian religions. Our theological task therefore is to see what role Christology could play in such religious situations with a view to discovering a constructive Christological approach to the Christian encounter with the religions in the East. Methodologically speaking we need to see, first of all, why Christology can be the central focus of our theological undertaking. And we can best do this by looking above all into our life of prayer.

"In the name of Jesus Christ", these are the words with which we conclude our prayers. By uttering these words we are giving witness to the reality of the inner and outer impacts which Jesus Christ makes upon us as our Mediator. He is the One who acts in His mediatorial office. He brings our sighs, desires and prayers to the throne of God's grace. He stands between God and man, being transparent to God on behalf of man. He is our access to God, for he is the Way (John 14.6). He lets our words merge into his Word as he exercises his High Priestly function before God. This is our experience of Jesus Christ as One who is active in the most secret part of our being. But there is a more objective side in our Christian experience. For time and again we are struck with wonder of the divine mystery when we read these words in John 1.14: "the Word became flesh and dwelt among us." Here is Jesus Christ, the primeval Word viewed *sub specie eternitatis*. This is the inexhaustibly profound reality of the eternal presence of Jesus Christ with God the Creator who on that very account could become present personally in the world which is God's creation. The emphasis at this point is to be laid on the verbs "became" and "dwelt". They express movement and settlement respectively. This action on the part of the Word of moving out from himself and of settling down in the world leads us to the dynamic synthesis which embodies in itself the purpose and goal of that action, namely, "God was in Christ reconciling the world to himself" (2 Cor. 5.19). This is the act of God's redemption realized and actualized in the "becoming" and "dwelling" of the Word among men.

It goes without saying that this is the vital stream running through the whole of St Paul's Christology. St Paul, no less than the writers of the synoptic Gospels, does not indulge in speculation upon the static nature of Jesus Christ. His Christology is a verbal Christology. For him it is always the living risen Lord that continually acts in and upon men and the world. An example can be cited to illustrate this. In the midst of exhorting the Corinthian Christians to be generous in their concern for the poor brethren in Jerusalem he bursts out spontaneously into a Christological confession: "For you know the grace of our Lord Jesus Christ, that though he was rich, yet for your sake he became poor, so that by his poverty you might become rich" (2 Cor. 8.9), which reminds one of the Christological hymn in the letter to the Ephesians 2.6–8. In these and many other concise but rich expressions St Paul visualizes for himself and for those he is addressing the divine redemption which has been materialized in and through Jesus Christ. God and the world, or God and man, have finally come to grips with each other in Jesus Christ. It is this dynamic character of Christology with its goal in redemption and reconciliation always in view that must become the pivotal point which keeps in unity varied phases of the Christian faith and which constitutes the gravitational pull in the life of Christians.

Out of these considerations we have arrived at one vital reality of the Christian faith, namely, Christology without soteriology would be empty, while soteriology without Christology would be blind. In Reinhold Niebuhr's words, in the New Testament "the Atonement is the significant content of the Incarnation."[25] That is to say, Christology and soteriology support and give meaning to each other. One cannot do without the other. The Word made flesh is the Lamb slain. The Word and the Lamb become united in one person of Jesus Christ in the redemptive will of God. The Word uttered becomes the Lamb slaughtered. This intimate soteriological relationship between the Word and the Lamb is no other than the relationship expressed between the person of Jesus Christ and his work. In other words, the person of Jesus Christ and his work form an inseparable totality in the redemptive love of God. We have to lay stress on this point again and again because, as we have seen, it is a separation of the work of Jesus Christ from his person that causes one of the basic Christological errors to happen in the East. Perhaps our own human experience will help us to understand a little the inseparability of person and work. It is true to say that a man's work is an expression, though partially and never fully and completely, of his person. As a matter of fact the person of a great artist lives on in his works. He pours out his whole person, or his whole being, in each piece of his artistic work in such a way that we can almost say that to see his work is to see his person.

Now what I am driving at is that the person of Jesus Christ is the ontological basis, to use a somewhat static term, of his redemptive and atoning work, while the redemptive and atoning work of Jesus Christ is the historical actualization or the existential embodiment of his person.[26] The Bible has taught us the plain truth that "who Jesus Christ is" can only be answered through perceiving and experiencing for ourselves "what he has done" for us men and the world, and that he is able to do what he has actually done solely on the ground of "who he is". To use another expression, the Being and Act of Jesus Christ are mutually interpretative because they belong together.[27] The Being of Jesus Christ will lose its immediate significance for us when considered in isolation from his Act. In the same way, the Act of Jesus Christ will lose its universal redemption and atoning power as soon as it is viewed in separation from his Being. The failure to recognize this essential fact drove the Pharisees and scribes to pour their anger upon Jesus Christ who, in their religious eyes, was nothing but a blasphemer of God. The same failure blinded the masses who wanted to see in Jesus Christ nothing but a miracle-worker or a hero-king. This divorce of the person of Jesus Christ from his work, and the divorce of his work from his person, also cause the non-Christians in the East to see in Jesus Christ either an incarnation among numerous incarnations or appearances of the Absolute, or an ethical teacher who has fulfilled his human nature through his moral perfection. Jesus Christ in the New Testament refuses to be subject to such a monstrous dichotomy. His divine authory consists precisely in the fact that his supernatural Being is in his Act. This is why those who heard him were astonished at his teaching, for "he taught them as one who had authority, and not as scribes" (Mk. 1.22). It is his Being in his healing Act that made the spectators say: "We never saw anything like this!" (Mk. 2.12). But our picture of Jesus Christ will remain a torso unless we are able to say in the same breath that his Act is in his Being. This is the reason why he had such breadth and depth of insight into human nature and human problems. It is on the ground of this Christological reality that we are not scandalized by his all too human actions. His association with sinful men and women, his shedding of tears for human misery, his compassion for those who gathered around him; these acts of his welled out of his very Being which is the incarnate Love of God made flesh and dwelling among men for their redemption and reconciliation.

On the same ground of his Being in his Act and his Act in his Being, we shall make a caricature of Jesus Christ if we split him into the Jesus of history and the Christ of faith, the split which has gone deep into the heart of theological controversies on Christology in the history of modern theology since the nineteenth century. D. M. Baillie who felt deeply the scandal of such dichotomous Christology rightly says: "If it is true that "no man can say, 'Jesus is Lord, except in the Holy Spirit', it is equally true that no man say it, in the true Christian sense, except through a knowledge of what Jesus actually was, as a humble personality, in the days of his flesh."[28] It seems, however, an inescapable defect of human nature not to be able to keep one's balance. In spite of his good intentions in trying to do justice to both sides and to steer a middle way with caution, Baillie is not altogether free from an adoptionist tendency in his great stress on the paradox of grace.[29] Perhaps this an indication that in dealing with Christology which is the central problem in Christian theology, we are standing on a holy ground where our static logicality ought to give way to adoration in joy and praise. If our Christology is a Christology concerned with the mystical union of God and man in one person, with the inseparable relationship between the essence and existence of that person, with the dynamic interdependence of his person and his work, and finally with his Being and his Act in mutual operation, history and faith must be kept in a creative tension, History is not just a series of contingent happenings which serve to invoke faith; while faith is no mere spiritual experience constantly relegating history to oblivion. History is not simply functional in the service of faith; while faith is not so autonomous as to be able to lord over history according to its own intention. Rather what we have in the Christian life is the historical faith in the dynamic synthesis of Being and Act, which is sustained, nourished, by the ultimate act of God's incarnating

Love. Jesus Christ is thus Being and Act in one person. The Being and Act of Jesus Christ becomes, in the communion of incarnating Love, the subject as well as the object of the historical faith of Christianity.

This last formula—Being and Act in the communion of incarnating Love—is thus our first Christological principle. Where the dynamic of this communion is rightly perceived and grasped, there we are led to the presence of the reconciling God in the person of the particular: a Jew called Jesus from Nazareth. On the contrary where the dynamic of this communion is set aside or lost sight of, there we are confronted with either a deified Jesus or a humanized Christ. It is very essential to keep this active, dynamic communion of incarnating Love in the Being and Act of Jesus Christ if we are not to fall into the Christological maze created by the theologians of the past and of the present on the one hand, and if we are to discover the rightful role of Christology in the Christian encounter with religions of the East. It does not mean that the classical Christological formula of the Nicene-Chalcedonian theology has lost its theological relevancy in our time. Jesus Christ as very God and very man, *inconfuse*, *inseparabiliter*, *immutabiliter*, and *indivise*, is forever the Jesus Christ of the Christian confession. It does, however, mean that if Christology is going to play a constructive role at all in the midst of religions in which salvation is regarded as either an attainment of the timeless Nirvana or as perfection of man's moral nature which is the Tao, mere repetitions of that traditional formula will not make Jesus Christ more real in any way to the people brought up in different religious traditions of the East. It does also mean that it cautions us against abstractly speculating upon the nature of Jesus Christ and thus failing to let the paradoxical reality of the incarnating Love take hold of our theological exercise. In view of this, D. N. Baillie aptly observes what Gwatkin says of Arius that he "never speaks of the love of God.'[30]

The second observation concerning the function of Christology is this. If we are able to see in the incarnating Love of God the active and organic communion of the Being and Act of Jesus Christ for the redemption and atonement of man and the world, it will naturally follow that any Christology which is content to remain as mere Christology is bound to become self-defeating. Since Jesus Christ is the primary datum of our Christological endeavour, we may have to see the point Nicolas Berdyaev makes when he says: "But philosophy and theology should neither start with God nor with man (for there is no bridge between these principles), but rather with the God-Man."[31] This statement, however, shows us only part of the total enterprise of God's redemptive work. We have to go on and say that "it is the person and work of Jesus Christ that raises most acutely the question and reality of God, of man, of the world."[32] If what we have said earlier in the above section is brought to bear upon our thinking at this point, we have to say that the incarnating Love of God manifested in the Being and Act of Jesus Christ calls into question our ideas and understanding about God, man, and the world. Just as Jesus Christ broke his own body in order that the brokenness of God's creation and creatures might be made whole again, so Christology has to break its narrow confinement in order that the light of Jesus Christ may shine in the darkness of man's understanding of God, of himself, and of the world. There is, in Christology, no abiding city for us to dwell in By virtue of the dynamic character derived from the Being and Act of Jesus Christ in the communion of the incarnating Love of God, Christology cannot help but move out from itself and show us who God is, what man is, and what the world is. This is something utterly strange to many religions in the East. They are not endowed with such a vital religious centre from which proceeds spontaneously and creatively the ever fresh and new revelation of God, in the light of which man is constantly brought face to face with new realities about God, man, and the world. As Kitagawa says of Buddhism, "there is no revelation or revealer behind Buddha's experience of Enlightment under the Bodhi tree. He found the secret of Good Law by himself. 'I have no teacher; none is like me; in the world of men and spirits none is my compeer. I am a saint (arahat) in this world, a teacher unsurpassable, the sole supreme Buddha.... And in the darkened world I will be the drum of the immortal'."[33] This is not only true of Buddhism, but also true of other religions in the East. That is why revelation has ceased to be a meaningful reality for them. There is nothing new under the sun.

The situation, however, has already begun to change. Under the impact of cultural and religious thoughts from the West, the people in the East have started to feel uncomfortable in remaining under the tyranny of Fate and have begun to stir themselves up from the bed of resignation. What they are desperately in need of at this historical juncture is visible and definite powers of an active supernatural being in whom their old *theo*-logy, *anthropo*-logy, and *cosmo*-logy, undergo redemptive and atoning trans-formations. They need a new theology, new anthropology, and new cosmology, in place of the old ones in order that they may become new men for the hope and future which are theirs in Christ. As a matter of fact, this kind of transformation has, to some extent, already taken place. But so far it remains at the superficial level. To be more exact, it is Christian humanism and Western science and technology that are largely responsible for any transformation which has been brought into existence. As Paul Tillich says: " ... in all Asiatic religions the indirect, civilizing influence of Christianity is, for the time being, decisive, and not its missionary work."[34] In other words, the direct and decisive encounter of Jesus Christ with Eastern religions has not yet taken place. Out of consideration of the situation such as this, we believe that there is almost insuperable advantage in viewing God, man, and the world through Jesus Christ in the way described above, for in Jesus Christ the Indian pantheistic faith and the Chinese concentration on humanism are brought face to face with the Christian reality of redemption and atone-ment. The Indian Nirvana will, thus, be called into serious question by Jesus Christ as the Being *in Act*, and the Chinese Tao will be exposed to the transcendent majesty of *the Being* in Act. Out of this religious encounter at its deepest level the pessimistic Indian view of the world as samsāra, as an everlasting round of beings circling from birth to rebirth, will be broken and redeemed by the dynamic action of God through his incarnating Love which is Jesus Christ, while the Chinese optimistic view of the world as having its own intrinsic comprehensive harmony will be shaken out of its self-sufficiency and complacency by that same divine reality which shows us profoundly the world in disharmony. This break-through has to be brought into being in the Christian encounter with religions in the East. In the true Christological sense, this break-through means death. But it is the death through which the event of resurrection will take place. Here the Pauline theology of baptism has a very significant rele-vance for us. In his letter to the Romans St Paul writes: "We were buried therefore with him by baptism unto death, so that as Christ was raised from the dead by the glory of the Father, we too might walk in newness of life." (Rom. 6.4.).

As is well known, the religious piety of Eastern people is almost proverbial. The Religious art of India and the Chinese art of

nature excel in beauty and spirituality. But until they have under-
gone the redeeming processes of death and resurrection in Jesus
Christ they remain alienated from God, exhibiting human nature
in its painful struggle for self-salvation. On the other hand, when
a real Christological transformation takes place within these
religions, then the latter will go through a kind of redemptive
emancipation which frees them from their bondage to their deities,
self, and nature. Through this redemptive emancipation resulting
from Christological confrontation the Chinese will be able to
intuit the meaning of the Incarnation in a most vivid and personal
way. In the Chinese language the words "love" and "pain" are
mutually exchangeable. Moreover these two words are combined
into making a verbal expression which expresses human love in
its highest degree. A mother "pain-loves" her child for example.
From our own human experience it is true to say that you have
not really loved someone until you feel pain in your love. For
when love and pain are mingled together in a single act, then
you really begin to love with the whole of your being. In your
"pain-loving" you pour out yourself for the person you love.
Your whole being goes out for that person. This is the kind of
love exhibited in the father of the prodigal son. In their religious
systems, however, the Chinese seem not to be able to bring their
human experience of "pain-loving" to bear upon their religious
experience of the supernatural, or Heaven. Heaven in Chinese
thought, apart from its naturalistic association with the sky, is
usually taken to mean "Imperial Heaven Supreme Emperor",
which is the supreme presiding power of the universe or the
ethical first principle of the world.[35] It is incapable of self-
sacrificial love accompanied by pain. Perhaps this is one of the
reasons why the Chinese took to Buddhism, especially Mahāyāna
Buddhism, which promised to offer them salvation through the
merits of Bodhisattvas. But Jesus Christ is not a Bodhisattva. He
is God's pain-loving *enmanned*. When we see Jesus Christ we see
God who acts for us, who does not spare himself in the Being
and Act of his own Son. Jesus Christ shows us the God who is
capable of pain-loving for the sake of mankind. For the Chinese
Jesus Christ is the pain-loving of the absolute God incarnate. In
him, and in him alone, human nature is both rejected because
of its alienation from God and fulfilled because it is fulfilled for
us in Jesus Christ.

A similar thing can be said of Hinduism. Its principal religious belief is expressed very well in the following words: "Endless change without, and at the heart of the change an abiding reality —Brahman. Endless change within, and at the heart of the change an abiding reality—Atman. Were there then two realities? No, answered ṛṣis,[36] Brahman and Atman are one and the same. And they summed up the prodigious affirmation in the words Tat Tvam asi—That thou art."[37] This identification of the Atman with Brahman which constitutes the major theme of Hindu thought from the very beginning resulted in regarding salvation as Self (Atman)-realization. This is the so-called Mokṣa, liberation from the physical individual self and attainment of the state of desirelessness in which the Self or Atman is wholly absorbed and extinguished in the infinite oneness with the Brahman. In such a religious system there is little room for the acting love which is willing to redeem, atone, and reconcile. Since there is no such acting love, the question of sin and forgiveness does not arise between the Atman and Brahman. There is only "ignorance" (avidyā) on the part of the individual self which creates problems for the Atman in its ascetic effort to be merged into mystical oneness with Brahman. This contempt for the individual self as the seat of "ignorance" has amounted to depersonalization of man in many Eastern countries in which Indian religious thoughts, whether in the Hindu or in the Buddhist form, have gained influence. In many Eastern societies one of the hardest things in human relationships is to forgive and to be forgiven. This is understandable because, ultimately speaking, forgiveness is a reality which can only happen between a person and another person. Apart from personal relationships, forgiveness cannot be exercised and experienced. According to the Bible, this depersonalization or dehumanization of man is the result of man's sinning against God who created him in his own image which would have enabled him to have personal relationship with God and with his fellow creature. But in Jesus Christ this depersonalized man is made a person again. He shows us the God who loves and forgives and redeems man, not in a metaphorical sense or in detachment, but in his own person and in immediate concreteness. Moreover Jesus Christ shows us the God who comes all the way to the East in the Being and Act of his own Son, not to condemn Eastern culture, but to judge and redeem it. This means a radical transformation for Eastern culture whose beauty and spirituality will be no more bent in upon itself but will be directed towards God in humility and praise saying:

And every virtue we possess,
And every victory won,
And every thought of holiness,
Are his alone.[38]

This means nothing more nor less than a new creation which
will come to body itself forth in a Christological *theo*-logy, a
Christological *anthropo*-logy, and a Christological *cosmo*-logy.

6

THE PROBLEM OF PAIN
IN CHRISTOLOGY[1]

KAZO KITAMORI

THE "PURPOSEFUL STRUCTURE"

In his essay "Towards an interpretation of the Second Clause of the Apostles' Creed"[2] Karl Holl has put forward the following important viewpoint: "In the second clause of the Apostles' Creed, namely in the confession of faith in 'Jesus Christ our Lord', a 'purposeful structure' ('planvolle Aufblau') may be found. In this may be seen 'the skill of the compiler' 'an inner form' or 'an overt theology', 'a remarkable and impressive structure'."[3]

We may ask what this has to do with the content to which the Apostles' Creed has given such a basic form. If we follow Holl it consists in the fact that, in the creed, the confession of faith in the "Lord" Jesus was "purposefully" connected with his *pain* and his *death*. One may of course say: "The death is really no proof of κυριότης"[4] (i.e. lordship), but the "skill" of the compiler and "an overt theology" consist (according to Holl) in the fact that the compiler makes the unusual and yet determinative connection between the idea of "Lord" and the death and passion. Holl's insight, to which we are indebted, is all the more noteworthy, when one considers that, although the Apostles' Creed is the most commonly used credal formula, the "purposeful structure" which is so determinatively incorporated is largely overlooked. One may ask whether this view unfolded in the treatment of the Apostles' Creed rings true within the situation of the Early Church, which the New Testament had produced. Even in the New Testament itself this "purposeful structure" may be perceived as an "overt theology". Our view of the early Church should tell us that the "skill" of the compiler belongs to an earlier period. For what is true of the Apostles' Creed is also true of the New Testament, where the concept of "Lord" is usually associated with the concept of "pain" in its basic mean-

ing. We may take it that the expression "the Lord of pain"
(which is in current use) is one which the compiler of the
Apostles' Creed deliberately took up. And yet this connection
of the concept "Lord" with that of "pain" is one which must be
constantly reviewed, for one finds here the basic problem of
Christology in respect of its content.

We may admit that in present-day theology much effort goes
into the phrasing of the content of Christology, and yet one
questions whether regard is given to the "purposeful structure".
In the essay I have quoted Holl has pointed out that pain stands
in specific contrast to the concept "Lord". It is precisely on this
point that the Christological problem must be resolved. If the
basic affirmation of faith in the "Lord" involves reference to the
pain of the man Jesus, the Church's Christological affirmation
for the first time becomes an "overt theology". It is on this point
that the Church's theological "purpose" must concentrate.
Inasmuch as Holl expresses the concept "Lord" by the Greek
$\kappa\nu\rho\iota\acute{o}\tau\eta\varsigma$, it could be said that the question of relationship is
only posed for Greek thought. It is, however, also a question for
Hebrew thought. In the latter, difficult questions arise. In the
Old Testament, God the "Lord" is deliberately associated with
pain. The following passages will serve for an example: "And
the Lord was sorry that he had made man on earth, and it
grieved[5] him to his heart" (Gen. 6.6). "When they suffered pain,
the Lord suffered too" (Isa. 63.9).[6]

Since the Jews regarded the Bible which incorporated these
texts as their Holy Scripture, one may take it that (for them)
the concept "Lord" is not necessarily in contradiction with the
concept "pain". Nevertheless, as Paul says, the "crucified Christ
was a stumbling-block to the Jews" (1 Cor. 1.23). Two reasons
may be given for this. In the first place, the inter-connection
between "Lord" and "pain" has been more consistently and more
profoundly made in the Christian Church than in Judaism. Holl's
comment on the "inner form" points to this more basic attitude.
The second reason is that the Christian Church has connected
the pain of God the "Lord" with Jesus of Nazareth. Even if one
allows that Judaism accepted a connection betweeen God and pain
in the Old Testament, it could hardly allow for this to be trans-
ferred to the historical figure of Jesus of Nazareth. This has
become 'a stumbling-block to the Jews.' An added cause for
bringing these two reasons together is the fact that from the
time of the Book of Daniel (which sprang from Jewish

Apocalyptic Literature) it had become normal to introduce the Messiah, now designated as the "Son of Man", as one possessing might and glory and utterly removed from pain and death (cf. Dan. 7.13f.)

If, however, we turn back again to Holl's assertion and look for a basis for the way of thought which sees a contradiction between the concepts "Lord" and "pain", it becomes obvious that it is to be found in the Greek rather than the Jewish way of thinking. It is the idea which we meet later in the form of God's *impassibility*. "It is understood that its origin lies in the influence of Greek philosophy. Because God is considered in his fundamental being to be unchanging, almighty, perfect and self-sufficient, it does not allow him to know pain which results from the lack of these qualities."[7] To the extent that, in recent times, there has been doubt expressed about the concept of divine impassibility,[8] one may also speak of the revival of the Jewish way of thinking as against the Greek. "If one takes it that divine impassibility is a doctrine dependent on the influence of Greek philosophy, in terms of the history of thought, one may affirm that the idea of divine possibility involves a revival of Jewish thought."[9] One may assert this because, at least in some passages of the Old Testament, God and pain are deliberately interconnected (Gen. 6.6; Isa. 63.9 etc.). Despite this, for the two reasons that I have adduced above (namely the profounder treatment given to the matter in the New Testament and the link made between the pain of God and the life of Jesus of Nazareth) the crucified Jesus was "a stumbling-block to the Jews".

The concept of κυριότης, lordship, then, does not allow itself to be associated with pain either in the case of Greek thought or yet in the case of Jewish thought. The very heart of Christology is reached where it breaks through that thick wall of partition and sees "Lord" and "pain" in substantial unity.

Our theme, the Problem of Pain in Christology, will require us to enter into a dialogue with Greek thought as represented above, but it will also require us to go further back and take up the dialogue with Jewish thought. It may be said that, since Paul understands the question according to the Jews as one which would be solved in the last stage of God's plan of salvation (Rom. 11.25f.), this fact should, theologically speaking, indicate the need for a basic dialogue with Jewish thought on Christology with especial reference to the theme of pain involved in it.

FROM THE STANDPOINT OF TIME

The Problem of Pain in Christology must next be treated from the standpoint of time, that is, as an historical problem. In the formulation of traditional Christology, this would mean from the standpoint of the "true humanity" (*vere homo*). Here our deliberations cannot but accept the form of an inter-debate between systematic theology (dogmatics) and biblical theology. Biblical theology cannot stand simply by its content, thus becoming biblical scholarship; inasmuch as it is biblical *theology*, it cannot stop short at positive, verifiable observations, but must quite obviously engage in debate with the systematic thinking we know as systematic theology. The reverse is also clearly true, that systematic theology (dogmatics), if it seeks to develop the relationship of its Christology to the "true humanity", must take up the thoughts and utterances of Jesus of Nazareth as the "true man" and therefore enter into discussion with the research of biblical theology. It is precisely dogmatics as systematic theology that must be stimulated by positive research. Were this essentially denied, Christology as a classical, dogmatic thought-product would probably be lost in abstraction. The "true man" who provides a determinative basis for the starting-point of Christology is actually a being who presents himself as an object for positive research. Dogmatics as systematic theology, in respect of the methodology it adopts in treating of the "true man", will certainly show a qualitative distinction from positive research, but it still has material *in common with* the latter, to which it applies itself, namely, the "true man" Jesus. This blending of what is "distinct" and what is "common" I call mediation.

Now if one tries to bring systematic and biblical theology together into debate, one can only avoid some of the obstacles with difficulty. Indeed, on the part of systematic theology it is impossible to find any uniformity of view, and despite the title "systematic" completely unsystematic relationships are to be observed. On the other hand, there is an even greater lack of uniformity of research in biblical theology and an even greater confusion with respect to questions concerning the relationship of the historical Jesus and the Church's theology. In this situation it will be necessary to search for the possibility of a new point of breakthrough. A parable may serve to explain this:– On the surface of the sea waves form with the blowing of the wind. If one were to direct one's attention to the movement of each individual wave, one could hardly avoid getting an impression of confusion. If, however, one were to look down on the sea from a helicopter or a plane, one could, despite the movements of individual waves, make out the form of the sea on a greater scale, perhaps in the form of a current of the sea. In this way, we would come to a commanding survey. In our real-life case, too, we have no other option than to adopt this attitude.

Seen from the standpoint of time, it is immediately clear that the man Jesus of Nazareth suffered and died on the cross. Inasmuch as time involves this fact, practically every positive assessment will serve to corroborate it. Theology must proceed from this fact. That the man Jesus of Nazareth suffered and died on the cross is an object of positive assessment (of evidences), a so-called historical fact. The peculiarity of historical events is that they are objective facts and are not immediately connected with the subject who makes the assessment. At least, they are not connected in a personal way. A personal connection I would call a *relationship*, but a relationship only comes into being between two personal beings. Impersonal beings have no relationship with one another. One cannot maintain a statement like the relationship between the tree and me. If the pain of Jesus of Nazareth is looked at from the standpoint of *time*, it becomes first and foremost an "historical fact". This is a fact which every positive assessment confirms, and which can stand without the faith of the subject. Since faith and theology have the understanding of Jesus of Nazareth as the "true man" in common with every positive assessment, they must both proceed from this fact. But this is no more than a "starting-point".

Faith becomes faith and theology becomes theology precisely at the point when the pain of Jesus, which up till now has been discerned as an historical fact as the result of positive historical assessment, is now understood *in a personal relationship* to the discerning subject. This personal relationship I would call "love". Love no longer allows the subject of the historical assessment to place himself outside the relationship. One may accept or reject this, but in either case there will have been an encounter in a personal way.

If I accept the pain of the "true man" Jesus in a personal relationship to myself as subject, then I have admitted that this love has a certain definitive character for me in terms of a personal relationship. The love of Jesus proves itself to me precisely as a *love through pain*. Hence, out of pain, out of the

Kazo Kitamori

pain of Jesus, which faith affirms in common with positive and historical assessment, there emerges for me in the assessment of faith a characterizing of the love of Jesus.

What has been expounded above represents the first step in Christological assessment. But from this stage there does not yet appear to "purposeful structure" to which Karl Holl has referred. We have been concerned with the pain and the death, but the concept "Lord", which is associated with them, has not yet come into the argument. The fact that both the Apostles' Creed and the New Testament possess a "purposeful structure" as an "overt theology" (to use Holl's language) means that the pain of Jesus, hitherto apprehended, is elevated from being the pain of the "true man" to being the pain of the "true God". This "true God" (*vere deus*) is none other than the "Lord". If the "inner form" of Christology is to be found in the connection between the "Lord" and "pain", then the view we have hitherto explored from the standpoint of time must now receive increased height and depth from the standpoint of eternity.

FROM THE STANDPOINT OF ETERNITY

The "purposeful structure" consistently pursued from the New Testament to the Apostles' Creed will be taken up from the Nicene Creed. This occurs in the connection between the confession of faith in the Lord and the pain. With a view to this structure we may see both a positive and a negative side in the Nicene Creed.

First, let us consider it from the positive side. I wrote earlier in this essay that "the very heart of Christology is reached where it sees 'Lord' and 'pain' in substantial unity, and it is the concept 'substance' which receives its classical form of expression in the Nicene Creed. It occurred in the statement that Christ was "of one substance with the Father" (ὁμοούσιος). The only-begotten Son Christ who is "of one substance with the Father" is the form of the Lord Christ who is worshipped from the standpoint of eternity. We shall speak later of the problems related to the concept of substance, but we will not go astray, if the original viewpoint of the Nicene Creed is characterized in passing, and the concept "Lord" seen from the standpoint of eternity with the aid of the concept "substance". Thinking of the confession of faith in the "Lord" from the standpoint of eternity certainly does not mean that one must understand the newly-introduced concept "substance" as "non-existential", especially since the love of Jesus, already revealed to us, is now comprehended as the love of the eternal God. If, however, the connection between the love of Jesus and the substance (being) of the eternal God were in principle rejected, then we should never arrive at all at an existential *theology* no matter how much we used the term "existential theology". Theology, as the word itself implies, is a science which has to do with God. Existential analysis is certainly a part of anthropology, but not theology. A correctly understood theology concerns itself with an enlightening of the relationship between the eternal God and man in his existence. In this it is through and through a matter of relationship. And because it is concerned with a relationship, human existence must necessarily be an ingredient. But the other aspect is also involved. Because it is concerned with a relationship, human existence must of necessity stand *vis-à-vis* God and the *real Other*. It is this relationship which "love" defines in concrete terms. The love which consists in a relationship between Jesus and ourselves refers now to the love of the "Lord" Jesus and proceeds from the being of the eternal God. The contribution of the Nicene Creed rests in the fact that it has identified in substance Christ's love for us and the love of the eternal God.

At the same time, however, we must indicate a negative aspect alongside this positive aspect. This is shown in the fact that the Nicene Creed is content simply to see Christ as the one "who took flesh", but strictly speaking provides no further development even in the context where it speaks of him as the one "who took pain". What is here taught about the pain of Christ only represents a repetition of the expressions used since the time of the Apostles' Creed, but recognizes no mode of expression such as the one which the compiler of the Apostles' Creed had deliberately applied. In this we may see the Latin character of the Apostles' Creed as opposed to the Greek character of the Nicene Creed. A feature of Greek thought is that fallen humanity will be preserved from destruction through the incarnation of the eternal Word and that redemption is consequently part of a conceived plan. As a result the pain of the redeemer loses its essential necessity. It is perhaps at this point that precise limitation of the Greek concept of "substance" needs to be uncovered. One may suppose that its metaphysical character has *per se* impeded its connection with pain. That the Nicene Creed, although on the one hand it has made clear the participation of the Incarnate one in the substance of the eternal God, has yet taken a step backwards from the "purposeful structure" (the connection of "Lord" with "pain") of the Apostles' Creed is much to be regretted.

For my next point I should like to turn my attention to the Chalcedonian Definition. In this Definition the "structure" is expressed as "truly God and truly man". The positive side of this statement of faith consists in the confession of faith in Jesus as the "true man", but a negative side may also be demonstrated. It consists in the fact that the connection of "God" and "man" in Christ are not expressed positively but in negative terms, when it says of the divinity and the humanity that they are "neither confused nor separated".

I should like in conclusion to take a look at Luther's understanding of the *communicatio idiomatum*. In this the divinity and the humanity have beome "neither confused nor separated" in Christ, but stand together in the *communicatio*. The pain is now not only stated of Christ as the "true man" but also of Christ as the "true God". "One should not believe or teach that Jesus Christ as the man or as humanity has suffered pain, but should teach as follows: As God and man are not here (i.e. in Christ) two persons, but one undivided person, one shall assert and teach that God and Man (God's Son) has indeed suffered for us".[10]

But a further development is necessary—not in the somewhat metaphysical and substantial direction illustrated by the *communicatio idiomatum* but in a direction more suited for faith and personalistic thinking, as will become clear in the following phrases I quote: "How does God save man? See, whoever will save another must himself go the way of pain. . . . It is a basic truth of Christian teaching that this also holds good for the saving action of God. This is basically the essence of love—to send oneself into pain, to sacrifice oneself and thereby to save others. God who for man's sake can take pain upon himself. . . . What else would be the Gospel we have from Christ?"[11]

7

ANANYATVA: THE REALIZATION OF CHRISTIAN NON-DUALITY

MARK SUNDER RAO

DARSANA AND SIDDHAANTA

VISION AND DOCTRINE

A common feature of Christianity and Hinduism is that each of these faiths has a body of revealed Truth and Fact, a corpus of given revelation, in their scriptures. On this scriptural basis the adherents of each of these faiths build their interpretations and doctrinal systems, whose authority and authenticity is valid only in so far as they remain faithful to the core of revelation. Sruti, the scripture, is thus the ultimate authority in matters of faith and all that flows from it. Hence the anxiety of all system-builders and commentators to prove that their particular interpretation or exposition is true to sruti.

Another similar feature is that while the formulators of doctrine take off, so to speak, from the same ground—the given corpus of revelation considered divine and inviolate—they land on different regions of varied conclusions as to its import, significance, and utility. Thus arise different schools of thought and sects, apparently at variance with one another.

The Upanisads, the Brahmasūtras, and the Bhagavadgita form the triple basis of the Vedaantin Hindus, while non-Vedaantins have the Vaisnava, Saiva, and Sākta Aagamas as their basic scriptural authority. The Christians consider the Bible, with the Old and New Testaments, as the principal basis of their creeds and confessions.

What is one to make of this phenomenon? Each system of doctrinal belief, the creed and confession among the Christians and the siddhānta among the Hindus, is considered as upadesa-sāstra, to be accepted on authority, in fatih, as sacrosanct. One may not question, examine, analyse the contents; nor may one, as it suits him, accept or reject parts of it. The confessions and the siddhāntas are integral wholes to be accepted as such, as adequate for faith and life.

It is claimed on behalf of each confession and siddhānta that its intention is to integrate man with God, neighbour, and the world and thus bring about peace, sānti, abhyudaya, progress. But it is nevertheless true, by and large, that the followers of such confessions and siddhāntas have tended to maintain their distinctions and even adopt a hostile attitude to those who differed from them. And if there has been a semblance of peace between the communities it has largely been due to forces of a secular order that impinged on them.

In the face of this situation frequent attempts were made to reduce the differences and promote mutual understanding. Of such attempts both among Christians and among Hindus, syncretism and eclecticism have been resorted to in the past, with apparent but brief success. The question instead of finding a solution remained insistent as before.

Discussing these points once with the late Prof. P. N. Srinivasachari, one time Principal and Professor of Philosophy at Pachaiappa's College, Madras, I was interested to learn that he himself had devoted much thought and had come to an answer which he offered me for what it was worth. He also gave me a coy of one of his earlier works: *The Synthetic View of Vedānta*.

In his conversations with me and in his book he made the point that in order to gain a conciliatory view of the various schools of thought—the siddhāntas—it is necessary to make a distinction between Darsana and Siddhānta. The word darsana means perception, vision of the ultimate truth, reality; the word siddhānta means reflection and resultant interpretation. The darsana, the vision of Reality and man's relation to it, remained constant, definitive, normative and final, whereas the siddhānta could be considered contingent, suggestive, tentative and *ad hoc* formulations of the former. He pointed out that the very fact that within a siddhānta itself—as for instance the Sāmkara-siddhaanta (advaita)—the contemporaries of Samkara like Suresvara and his successors like Padampāda and Vācaspati Misra had offered a variant of the advaita, significant in its differences from the position maintained by Samkara. And when we remember that a noted Advaitin like Madhusūdana Saraswati could go so far as to adopt bhakti as integral to advaita, it can be understood that no system of philosophic formulation is final and binding on all. The same may be said of siddhāntas other than Sāmkara. Thus it is to be noted that the primary thing is the darsana and the siddhānta is derivative, secondary. It is the darsana that is inviolate; the siddhānta is subject to development and alteration.

It was my good fortune to gain a similar insight in the late thirties when I used to spend a great deal of my spare time on the campus of the United Theological College, Bangalore. Here frequently my host, friend, and guide in studies was the Rev. Dr A. Marcus Ward whose private library happened to be one of the finest I had seen till then. Among Prof. Ward's books I happened on those by Prof. C. H. Dodd and the late Dr Nathaniel Micklem. The common theme of these authors seemed to me to be this: There was on the one hand the *kerygma*, the proclamation of the Gospel and on the other the *didache*, the teaching. The primary and plenary thing was the kerygma, while the didache was derivative and relative. On the one hand we had the given facts and truth of revelation; on the other, its explication to the believers and application to life's problems. A distinction of this nature was important to understand the later doctrinal development or confessional effort.

We can now appreciate how in recent decades there has been a movement, both in the Christian and the Hindu communities, to veer away from those aspects of thought or belief which kept sections of people apart; these aspects being the constricting confessions and siddhāntas. At the same time there was evident a movement toward what was considered a body of truth valued as revelation and inviolate.

Therefore it seems to me that the need arises for a reconsideration of the relative position of the kerygma and the confession among the Christians and the darsana and siddhānta among the Hindus. This rethinking is needed for the vitalizing of the inner life of the communities as also for a wider understanding of the religious experience among people at large.

In this connection it might interest the readers if I refer to what a recent book *Theological Discussions and Confessions; Developments in the Churches in Asia and Africa* offers:

All the confessions are relative and limited. They are co-ordinate with, but subordinate to, the Bible as the only infallible rule of Christian faith and practice. The confession is only an approximation and a relatively correct enunciation of the revealed Truth and can be amended owing to this characteristic; the Bible remains infallible. The Bible is the rule of faith whereas the creed is the rule of the doctrine. The Bible has thus a divine and absolute authority with the result that any higher value ascribed to symbols is out of place. Thus the relative value of creeds indicates the way for new creeds and confessions to come into being just as the existing ones did.

(G. C. Oosthuizen)

But a movement away from the confessions and siddhāntas would itself be barren if the vitalizing insights won from returning to the primary kerygma and darsana were not brought back into the life of the community which cannot altogether do away with the confessions or siddhāntas: indeed they are unavoidable, for any result of reflection on the kerygma, darsana, would itself be incipient or potential confession, siddhānta.

But this question of a dual movement, away from and towards the confession and siddhānta, is of interest to those who in our day seek to promote a dialogue between the Christians and Hindus. For a Siddhānta provides a springboard for dialogue, though, as we have seen above, it is not at the Siddhānta level that we meet with the core of reality, but at the darsana level. Beginning at the Siddhānta level inevitably, the dialogue should be lifted to the darsana level where those involved in it comfort one another most truly because they are there face to face with reality. That is where the dialogue can reach the sharpest point.

Since, however, a dialogue between the Christians and the Hindus is important not only as a missionary venture but also for the wellbeing of the society as a whole, a pursuit of thought along the lines suggested by these paragraphs may help.

At this point we shall turn to the essential revelation of the Kerygma and Vedānta, bearing upon the aim of life of man as intended by his Creator. This aim, the goal of existence has already been adverted to as *perichoresis*—coinherence of the divine and human, the sahaja sāyujya as the Christians and Hindus in turn might tell us.

It is not intended in this monograph to run the entire gamut of Christian theology or Vedānta philosophy. It would be presumptuous to do so and impossible for the present writer. What, on the other hand, seems to be possible and appropriate is to deal with that aspect of thought pertaining to the stated end or aim in life, without cruising over related areas, however important they may appear to those who think further on the theme Ananyavāda.

TATTVA—ITS NATURE

ULTIMATE REALITY

Earlier I proposed that the subject matter of this monograph be divided according to the Hindu scheme, into tattva, hita, and purusārtha, i.e. the nature of the ultimate reality, the apprehension of its import and significance, and the consummation of an appropriate relation with it. A severe goal orientation of the Aacāryas, is of course, one reason for this division. The other and equally compelling reason is that it arises from the very nature of the spiritual aspirant's reflective self. That is, the self in the act of reflection is engaged with reality, in an endeavour to know its truth, and both with a view of ordering all life in accord with it, which is the value and the logical fruition of such activity. By its nature, therefore, spiritual reflective self appears to be goal or value oriented.

I suggest further that the central vision and doctrine both of Christianity and Hindu Vedānta are such as to provide precisely for this procedure. If we take the two doctrines, that of the Trinity for the Christians and the doctrine of the Brahman for the Hindus, to be fundamental to these two faiths and supposing a spiritual aspirant's reflection is devoted to them, how can one find a justification for these goal or value-oriented patterns of our subject matter into tattva, hita, and purusārtha?

Let us, for the present purpose, say that in the apprehension of God as Trinity (Father, Son, Holy Spirit) on the one hand, and the apprehension of Brahman as Sat, Cit, and Ananda on the other, it would appear that a spiritual reflective self thus engaged is at the same time engaged with reality, truth, and value. To put this in another way, Being, Sat, is the knowable; Truth, Cit, is knowledge; Value, Ananda, is the consummation of the process of knowing. If then we consider the systematic reflection to reckon as philosophy, the reflective self's task is to "determine in what consists the truth of knowledge, the reality of the knowable, and the value of the knowable and knowledge", as Prof. Alfred Stern put it. Philosophy is, or should be, goal-oriented no less than theology. So much for the presentation of the theme.

Engaged, thus, in the act of reflection as were the Aacāryas and the Church Fathers, it is plain from their writings that they were wary of such occupation for its own sake; they discourage it by emphasizing the ultimate mystery of the Godhead or the Brahman. The ultimate reality, they say, is aprameya, not an object of thought; it is avāngmanasāgocaram, inaccessible to word and thought; it is param, they beyond or the transcendent; it is the guhyam, the tremendous secret. And yet both the Aacāryas and the Fathers claim that there is a self-disclosure, a revelation from the Beyond effected "in the cave of the heart", intuited and known and intimately experienced with an over- whelming certainty. From such revelatory experiences arise darsanas, direct knowledge of its nature. In the nature of the case what may at first appear as definitions of the Divine and truly evocations of it.

As an example of this procedure we could cite a recent work of Prof. M. Yamunicarya of "The Teaching of Ramanuja in His Own Words". After the needed introductories he goes on straight through tattva, hita and purusārtha, appending at the end Aacārya Ramanuja's succint philosophical statement Saranāgati- gadya. To any one with a deep desire to understand and to share spiritual experience the book provides suggestive matter. I might also say the same thing about Saint Jnānesvara whose Amri- tānubhava is so planned that step by step it brings the reader to a spontaneous participation of thought and experience of the specific divine-human relationship arising from his particular siddhānta and darsana.

Lastly, let us take the very names of the siddhāntas, for example, advaita, visistādvaita, and dvaita. The very words are suggestive of a relation in which the divine and the human stand to each other. So it cannot be overstressed that all that we have so far stated goes to show how consistently and insistently goal- oriented the thinking of the Aacāryas has been, and if I under- stand efforts of the early Church Fathers, though their doctrinal expositions were made with reference to certain historical changes and challenges, the fact remains that in as much as their reflection was directed toward drawing forth an understanding of the nature of distinction and unity in the Trinity and the Incarnation they, so to speak, offered material to effect just such an evocation of direct, firsthand anubhava, experience that the Hindu Aacāryas intended to effect in their works.

Now we might take a brief look at the central insights of the

Hindu siddhāntas before turning to the similar Christian insights:

Advaita: Aatmā ca Brahma, the self is not other than Brahman. Reality cannot be two. The wrong notion of the self's being *other* or *anya* to Brahman causes bondage and the shedding of this notion through Jnāna, right knowledge, is moksha, salvation.

Visistādvaita: the self is an amsa, a part of the Brahman who is the amsin, the whole. There is a kind of difference as well as non-difference, as between parts and the whole. This intimate relation is called aprathaksiddhi, inseparability, integrality.

Dvaita: there is only one ultimate, independent, svatantra-reality: the Brahman. The other "reals", the man and the world, are utterly dependent, paratantra. The existence of the latter cannot be conceived apart from the former. To realize the relationship of such dependence is moksha.

Saiva Siddhānta: The individual selves are considered to be finite manifestations of the Creative Energy, Sakti of God, and are the integral parts of the divine being. This is a special form of advaita in as much as the relationship is described as abheda or non-difference.

We could, of course, mention a score of other siddhāntas; but that will not add to what we have said so far, because it may be taken that these four concepts are adequate as examples to understand the point of this section of the monograph.

Here, again, let us note that though the object of the Aacāryas is to point to an intimate relation between the divine and the human, in trying to spell out the import of it they take divergent courses. The late Prof. P. N. Srinivasachari has this situation in mind when he remarks:

> The relation between Brahman and Aatman is to be conceived not in terms of cause and effect, substance and quality, whole and parts which after all are categories of our under-standing. The analogies of the soul and the body, light and its luminosity, the flower and its fragrance are but devices of the intellect to portray the unity of the Aatman and Brahman and their union.

What really matters is to grasp the fact of such a relationship as being intimate, integral and eternal. The systematic expositions of the implications of this primary and plenary relationship is the task of the siddhāntas of the Aacāryas and these siddhāntas, as we have seen, lead people to think that there are "many

G

truths"; they confuse mata=opinion with tattva=truth, reality.

For this reason it is constantly impressed on spiritual aspirants that they should turn, at intervals, from the siddhāntas to the darsanas, the primary and plenary revelation in the sruti, the scripture. The darsana, sāksaat kāra, svaaunbhava—these terms are interchangeable—stand for intuitive, intimate, interior experience and find utterance in cryptic phrases like Aham Brahmāsmi, Ayam Aatma Brahma, Tat Tvam Asi, and Sarvam Khalvidam Brahma. These mahāvaakyas indicate no more than the integral relationship; they do not explain how it operates. This seems to suggest that it is not at the level of the siddhānta that we can gain an insight into the divine human relationship, but only at the level of the darsana. In other words it is anubhava as embodied in the sruti that should be the prime concern of the aspirants. Opinions, mata or systems of interpretations, the siddhāntas, are secondary, though important at their own level.

Again, the words darsana, vision, sāksaatkaara, realization, and anubhava, experience indicate immediacy, presence, and presentation whereas the word siddhānta, doctrinal system, indicates a posterior reflection upon the prior experience and mediacy, a representative character. The latter, therefore, is a derivative and a consequent activity of the reflective self and is, so to speak, a spectator's viewpoint. To the experient, on the contrary, anubhava, experience, is an involvement, and an interpenetration such as can be suggested or evoked by terms like ananyatva or perichoresis. It must be said, in spite of this distinction and criticism of the siddhāntas, their ultimate object remains that the aspirant should have his own darsākshaatkaara and svaanubhava.

Turning to the Christian faith, what do we find? Recent scholarship has tended to separate in the scripture itself what is termed as the kerygma and what is termed as didache, the proclamation of the revealed truth and the exposition and the teaching of it. This is somewhat akin to the call away from the siddhāntas and toward the darsana as in the case of the Hindus as shown above. The Church Fathers, too, regarded man's union with the divine as the end and aim of life. In the course of its history Christianity has offered several patterns of this union—*unio mystica*, *theosis*, *perichoresis*, and so on. They differ, like the Hindu Aacāryas, as to how this relationship can be spelled out; they agree, nevertheless, that it is reality that matters to the believer more than anything else.

From the various attempts made by the thinkers, Hindu and Christian, to explain how the two parties, so to speak, the divine and the human, are related, it may be discerned that it is done at several levels of existence and experience. It may be conceived at the transcendental level of the Being, i.e., at the ontological level. It may be conceived at the level of the creation, that is the cosmological level. It may be conceived at the level of the empirical man; then it would be an anthropological process. It may be conceived at the immanental level; then it would be pneumatical relationship.

In the Sāmkara vedaanta, for instance, it is held that ātma (jiva) is Brahman. Not indeed that the empirical jiva, be clouded, as it were, by advidyā-maayaa; but the one as a result of appropriate sādhana, divested of it. The intuition of oneness is said to be at the transcendental or ontological level. That is, the oneness of jiva and the Brahman, Brahmajivaikya, is discerned at the pre-biographical, pre-cosmological level whereby the jiva inheres in the uncreated and unrelated divine self. (A criticism of this claim appears later.) In the theistic thought, in the Saiva Siddhānta, for instance, the union with the divine is conceived at the cosmic level, that is a part of the process beginning with srishti through sthiti, samhāra, tirodhaana, and anugraha— creation, sustainment, annihilation, concealment, and manifestation of grace, in the union of the divine and the human. Then we are familiar with the yoga, the word itself meaning bringing together, union, which, from the standpoint of Sāmkhya Yoga school, can only mean a human achievement; being a purely psychic discipline and phenomenon it may without undue hesitation be termed an anthropological concept, and justifiedly so because the concept of Isvara (god) is an adventitious afterthought, so to speak. Lastly there is the concept of the human-divine relation conceived at the level of the immanent spirit, distinct from the human being, but inseparable from it. While the Hindu thought courses over all four dimensions, the more familiar concepts are rooted in one or another of the first three dimensions. But the peculiar contribution of the early Church Fathers is in the last dimension, as we shall presently see. It is because of the following factors. Inheriting their faith from Israel they believed in the solity and mystery of the Godhead whose inner being is unreachable; it rose from the conviction that though the creation had issued from God's act and really had him for its cause and ground of being, this fact did not, so to speak, guarantee the union of the human and the divine, as the empirical (fallen) life so amply illustrates; it arises from the conviction that "no man by taking thought can raise himself" to the divine, so that no psycho-physical operation can effect a union of man with God.

In other words, the Christian Fathers set aside theories of the divine-human union at the ontological, cosmological, and anthropological levels and reached out of the fourth dimension—that of the Indwelling Holy Spirit, the revealer within of the Incarnate Word, the Son who is the image of the Father. It is, perhaps, this almost exclusive emphasis which renders the position of the Church Fathers unique and suggests the distinction of the Christian thought in relation to the Hindu.

It may also be pointed out, for the purpose of this monograph, that the entire thought of the early Church Fathers moves between two axes, namely the Trinity and the Incarnation. But in spite of this almost exclusive emphasis on these two doctrines, in the undertone is the fact that it was the third Person of the Trinity, the Holy Spirit, the Indweller, that effected the mystical union, sāyujya, of God and man. It is thus, it seems to me, that the Church Fathers' concept of *unio mystica*, *theosis* or *perichoresis* ceases to be ontological or cosmological or anthropological but is pneumatical, if this usage be permitted. The "great divide", therefore, comes about between the first three concepts on the one side and the last on the other.

Having drawn the line of demarcation between the basic positions of the early Church Fathers and the Hindu Aacāryas it is still necessary to attempt another clarification. This pertains to what may be distinguished as the hypostatic union and mystic union of the divine and the human or to use another familiar terminology, *unio hypostatica* and *unio mystica*. A prima facie interpretation of the position of Samkara, it seems to me, is a form of *unio hypostatica*, that is one at the ontological dimension signified by the phrase Aatmā ca Brahma. But a deeper examination reveals a different position. He himself is aware that in this relationship there is Brahman on the one hand and Aatmā, jiva, on the other; the first is antahkarana rahita and the second is antahkarana sahita. Given the concept of Avidyā-maayaa that is responsible for the latter manifestation, it would seem that the antahkarana rahita Brahman and the antahkarana sahita ātman (jiva) fall into two categories, rendering it impossible to effect a union at the level of Being, an ontological unity. In the intuition of oneness, unity, there is bound to be the awareness which can only be spelled out as "There are two, but *they* are not two." In other words Sāmkara advaita seems to offer hypostatic union with one hand and mystic union with the other. That seems to be the meaning of the two sattās, realities—the paaramaarthika and the vyāvahaarika. In conclusion, since this analysis precludes ontological union of the divine and the human, the way is open for a pneumatological union, *unio mystica, perichoresis*, which we shall presently explain

Another important feature of the thought processes of the early Church Fathers is what may be called the societary character as distinct from the individualistic nature of Hindu thought processes. The distinction springs from the sources of the two faiths. Having taken over from Israel the belief of a whole nation, an entire community, called to be his own, the ultimate purpose of God being the creation of a community at one with him, it is but natural that theirs should be a society outlook as against an individualistic outlook. In the other case the upanisadic context of secret individual teaching, followed by private pursuit of what were once known as vidyās and now as yogas, tended to make the Hindu thought run along individualistic lines. It may be pointed out, of course, that there has been a tradition of sarva mukti; but on the face of it is not as a community but seriatim that the total mukti takes place; it is a far cry from the believers being a Mystical Body of Christ, a corporate spiritual entity.

Having established the distinction of the Christian outlook we can proceed to the specific darsana of the early Church Fathers. It may be remembered that this monograph is severely restricted to the divine human relationship; a cruise over the entire range of Christian doctrine is not called for.

THE TRINITY AND THE INCARNATION

Of the many doctrines of the Christian faith which comprise the Christa-darsana, the two—those mentioned above—are chosen for the light they throw on Christian non-dualism, ananyatva, which is our thesis. It will be seen that, in the explanation of the import of the two doctrines, the early Fathers were concerned with rebutting monism on the one hand and pluralism on the other.

The Trinity

The Church Fathers firmly affirmed, above all, the ultimate

mystery of the Godhead. He is for ever the hidden God. His hiddenness, however, is a correlative to his being a self-disclosing, self-revealing God. He is, in his essence, aprameya and cannot be made an object of thought; he is avāngmanasaagocaram, inaccessible to word or thought. He is the totally transcendent One; he is also the totally immanent One. These two poles were gripped and held together in all their thinking.

The plenary revelation is offered to us in the Trinity: the Father and the Son and the Holy Spirit. There are three and yet *they* are one. How is this to be understood—their being distinct and united? In clarifying this problem they made the way clear to understand the divine human-relationship that ensues.

It is a well known fact to students of early Church history that the Church Fathers solved this problem by the use of the words *hypostasis, ousia,* and *perichoresis.* They said that "the Three coinhere in One Another without coalescing, each possessing a perfect hypostasis and yet maintaining one ousia." The word they used for his coinherence is *perichoresis.* The Three are One and in that oneness they preserve their separate identity.

They seemed to have used the concepts of the species and the genus. According to this the three members of the Trinity belong to distinct species while it is the genus that constitutes their unity. In this line of thinking the species corresponds to *hypostasis* and the genus to *ousia.* Hypostasis is roughly rendered Person and ousia substance, nature. Thus the three Persons of the Trinity remain distinct while being one. The resulting insight into this relationship and status they expressed in the word *perichoresis,* coinherence. In this way, incidentally, the Fathers fought off, if we may say so, rigid monism and pluralism and affirmed what may be called non-dualism, anayavāda: There are three Persons: they are not three: they are One. This built-in concept of distinction in unity is the norm not only of relationship *in divinis* but of relationship divine and human, as we shall presently see.

The Incarnation

Following the treatment of the doctrine of the Trinity they interpret the divine and human natures in the Incarnation with the concept of *perichoresis.*

The divine and human natures are distinct and have specific properties, but in the Incarnate Person they interpenetrated, coinhered, in such wise that he is a man and God at the same time. This interpenetration, coinherence of the divine and the human, is brought about, according to the Church Fathers, in a certain sequence. First there is the penetration of the divine nature into the human and then that of the human into the divine.

An accurate translation of *perichoresis* would therefore be penetration or indwelling. The *perichoresis* is mutual, but always in the sequence as stated above. But the fact that the human nature assumed in the Incarnation is not the common fallen humanity, but the one already penetrated by the divine, divinized, the union of the divine and the human in the Incarnation is a hypostatic union, at the ontological level. Therefore a hypostatic union such as is manifested in the Incarnation is unrepeatable and unsharable, because the other human beings, according to the teaching of the Fathers, having lost the "image of God in them" through the Fall, can aspire to be taken into a divine-human relationship that may properly be called *unio mystica* as distinguished from *unio hypostatica* of the divine and the human in the Incarnation. Though there is this important distinction between the two forms of union there is still the common experience of *perichoresis*, mutuality, which cancels the ultimate dualism of the divine and the human on the one hand, and on the other creates a oneness of the two. The ensuing relationship can, it seems to me, be termed non-dual or ananyatva. According to this way of understanding the two doctrines of Trinity and the Incarnation we can, I believe, correctly claim for the Christian believer a non-dualist theology and philosophy. These two doctrines are, I believe, the charter of Christian non-dualism or Ananyatva. Hence we derive Ananyavāda, Philosphy of Non-Dualism.

It would seem that in the thinking of the early Fathers these two doctrines assumed greater importance than any other. For instance, the doctrine of the Holy Spirit, it is said, was still unexplored territory then as it is now. But the need to understand the idea of *perichoresis* drove the Christians to give more attention to the doctrine of the Holy Spirit.

The Holy Spirit

The *perichoresis* relationship, ananyatva, of God and man, offered, as the Church Fathers believed, (Irenaeus, for instance) in the very nature of the Godhead, could be brought about only by the working of God in man. No man could go to the Son except the Father; no effort of man would avail. But the One who uttered these words also assured that Another would come, the Paraclete, the Spirit who would impart the teachings of the Son and lead them into all truth and bring to fruition the divine-human relationship pictured by the Son in his prayer to the Father. In this way it came to be believed that in all creative and redemptive activity the Holy Spirit figured as "the Chief Executive" of the Godhead.

From the beginning to the end the dependence of the Christian believer on the Holy Spirit was complete and in the bringing about of a new creation, a new community of men who experienced the at one-ment with God and man, in offering to each member and the whole community the status of ananyatva, the role of the Holy Spirit was considered supreme. It should be remembered, however, that God is impartible and yet the Trinity functions in distinctive ways.

If, as been done by some, the three Persons of the Trinity may be said to embody three aspects of divine nature, namely, transcendence, revelation, and immanance, it may be said too, that the Holy Spirit is the effectualization of the immanence of God in man and creation. He is thus the real Antaryāmin, Indweller. And if it is remembered that the accurate translation of the word *perichoresis* is indwelling it may be taken that in the Holy Spirit there is both the promise and the guarantee of ananyatva, non-duality, resulting from *perichoresis*.

We have already suggested that the Christian view of life is not individualistic but societary in nature. Thus the believers held that by the operation of the Holy Spirit, the grace of the Lord Jesus Christ and the love of God were made fruitful so that they yielded their individualistic, separative, exclusive nature and were built together in one bundle of life with God through Christ by the Holy Spirit. Since such is the origin of the community and collectivity, of their union and mutuality, of their distinctness and oneness (i.e., the very Godhead), the tattva (= the nature of the resultant Church) is at once a mystery and a manifestation. It is a mystical Body of Christ whose oneness with its Head is manifest and hidden; promised as well as fulfilled; here and now, but far away, at the same time.

In this connection it is hard to forget the late Mr Pandipeddy Chenchiah who in his conversations at the Verandah Club and in his serious writings never tired of saying that it would be expected of India to develop a yoga of the Holy Spirit and to look for a new creation in Christ through the same Spirit.

It remains for me to recapitulate the idea of this section. We began with brief statements of the central teachings of a few Hindu siddhāntas. In a similar way we tried to understand the two Christian doctrines. In both cases we tried to remember that we were concerned with the divine-human relationship understood as nonduality or ananyatva and saw how this view found a basis in the teaching of the early Church Fathers and the Aacāryas.

NOTES

INTRODUCTION

1. R. Panikkar, *Das Kerygma und Indien*, Hamburg 1967; *Christus als unbekannter im Hinduismus*. Basel 1965.
2. The following are exceptions: H. Bürkle, *Dialog mit dem Osten*. Stuttgart 1965; H. Vogel, "Die Mystik Radhakrishnans und das Evangelium von Jesus Christus", in *Evangelische Theologie* 1961, pp. 387ff; O. Wolff, *Mahatma und Christus*, Berlin 1955; *Radhakrishnan*. Göttingen 1962; *Christus unter den Hindu*. Gutersloh 1965.
3. K. Kitamon, *Theology of the Pain of God*, S.C.M. Press 1966.
4. Compare for example *The Discussion in Helsinki*, the official Report of the fourth assembly of the Lutheran World Federation. Berlin 1965.
5. F. Lüpsen, *Neu-Delhi Dokumente*. Witten 1962, especially section II, pp. 41 ff., and Devanandan, *Zu Zeugen berufen*, 276; *Appell an die Kirchen der Welt*. Dokumente der Weltkonferenz für Kirche und Gesellschaft. Stuttgart 1967.
6. J. Rossel, *Dynamik der Hoffnung*, Basel 1967.
7. Ibid. p. 44.
8. K. Cragg, "Die Glaubwürdigkeit des Christentums", in *Okumenische Diskussion*, Genf 1967, Vol. III, No. 2, p. 67.
9. Harvey Cox, *The Secular City*, Penguin 1968, and A. Th. van Leewen, *Christentum in der Weltgeschichte*, Stuttgart 1966.
10. J. E. Y. Cheng, *Asian Conference on Church and Society*, Seoul 10–16, October 1967, Korea.
11. W. C. Smith, *Der Islam der Gegenwart*, Frankfurt 1957, Fischer-bücherei 498.
12. K. Baago, "The Post-Colonial Crisis of Missions", in *The International Review of Missions*, London, July 1966, pp. 331ff.
13. W. Elert, *Zwischen Gnade und Ungnade*, München 1948, pp. 78ff.
14. S. J. Samartha, *The Hindu View of History*, Bangalore 1959.
15. G. Rosenkranz, "Fernöstliches und Christliches Zeit—und Geschichts—Verständnis", in *Religionswissenschaft und Theologie*, München 1964, pp. 162ff.
16. W. Freytag, *Reden und Aufsätze*, München 1961, Vol. I, p. 173.
17. Ibid. p. 109.

18. U. Wilkens, "Ungebrochenes Reden von Gott" in *Radius* (Stuttgart) 1961, p. 15.
19. Kenneth Cragg, op. cit., p. 71.

CHAPTER 1

1. Paul Lehmann: "Que está haciendo Dios en el mundo", ("What God is doing in the World") (Buenos Aires, *Cuadernos Teologicos*, X/4, October–December 1961, pp. 243–68).
2. e.g. "Un Dios que actúa y transforma la historia", ("A God who acts and transforms history"), (*América Hoy*, Report of the ISAL Conference at El Tabo, Chile, 1966: Ediciones ISAL, Montevideo, 1966; pp. 57–70).
3. *Tierra Nueva*, I (1), October–November 1966, pp. 1, 5.
4. cf. Jer. 14.14; 27.15.
5. "La actualidad del fenómeno profético" ("The Reality of the Prophetic Phenomen"), Cuadernos Teologicos, Buenos Aires, XV/1, January–March 1966, pp. 63–75.
6. James Barr: *Old and New in Interpretation*, SCM Press, London 1966, esp. chapters 1, 3, and 6.

CHAPTER 3

1. *Udana, 80 Inspiring Words of the Buddha* (in *Sutta Pitaka, Khuddaka Nikaya*). A New Version by Bhadragaka, Bangkok 1954.
2. *A Faith for This One World?* p. 19. SCM Press 1961.
3. See *Cosmos and History, The Myth of the Eternal Return* by Mircea Eliade, p. 52 (Harper Torchbooks).
4. *ibid.*, p. 102.
5. *The Interpreter's Dictionary of the Bible, article* "Wrath of God".

CHAPTER 4

1. I am only at the beginning of my research in this field, so that what follows here is not more than an undigested outline which is far from being adequate.
2. For example: O. Cullmann: *Die Christologie des Neuen Testaments* (1957); F. Hahn: *Christologische Hoheitstitel* (1963); W. Kramer: *Christos, Kyrios, Gottessohn. Studien zur paulinischen und vorpaulinischen Christologie* (1962); E. Schweizer: *Erniedrigung und Erhohung bei Jesus und seinen Nachfolgern* (1962); V. Taylor: *The Names of Jesus* (1953), to mention only a few of the numerous books on this subject.
3. "Independent Churches" in Africa can be compared to sects in Europe which have broken off from the main state Churches. There are well over 2,500 of these separate or independent Churches in Africa, nearly all from the non-Roman Catholic denominations

(with one or two exceptions). The one studied by Turner is known as the "Church of the Lord (Aladura)", founded 1930.

4. A good study of these myths is made by H. Baumann, in his monumental work: *Schöpfung und Urzeit des Menschen im Mythus der afrikanischen Völker* (1936 and 1964).

5. D. Forde, ed., *African Worlds*, (1954), pp. 85ff., 162.

6. R. F. Gray: *The Sonjo of Tanganyika* 1963.

7. Cf. J. Jeremias: *Abba: Studien zur neutestamentlichen Theologie und Zeitgeschichte* (1966).

8. The literature on this is vast, but one of the old but illuminating books is by W. Bousset: *Kurios Christos* (1921).

9. Forde, op. cit. pp. 217, 220.

CHAPTER 5

1. Karl Barth, *Church Dogmatics* 2/1, p. 257.

2. See Rudolf Bultmann, "The Christological Confession of the World Council of Churches" in his *Essays, Philosophical and Theological*.

3. See George S. Hendry's article, "An appraisal of Brunner's Theology" in *Theology Today*, Vol. XIX, No. 4 (January 1963), p. 529.

4. Kurt Goldammer, *Die Formenwelt des Religionen*, 1960, pp. 45f: "Auf eine enfache Formel gebracht, kann man also das Ziel allen Religionen das 'Heil' bezeichen. Religion ist stets Heilsverheissung, die dem Menschen von Augen gestellt, und Heilweg, der ihm dargeboten wird." Cf. also H. F. Rall, *Religion as Salvation*, 1953, p. 87: "Salvation is the focal point of religion." Paul Tilich says the same thing in his own way: "Das Verlangen nach einem Neuen Sein ist universal, weil die menschliche Entfremdung universal ist. Das Verlangen nach dem Neuen Sein ist in allen Religionem zu finden." (*Systematische Theologie*, Vol. 2, p. 96).

5. Joseph M. Kitagawa, *Religions of the East*, 1960, p. 148.

6. Radhakrishnan, *Recovery of Faith*, 1955, pp. 13f.

7. It must be noted that what Radhakrishnan means by "the essential truths of all religions" are the teachings taught in different religions. In his earlier book, *Eastern Religions and Western Thought*, 1939, he produces parallel teachings of Buddha and Jesus in a skilful fashion, cf. pp. 173ff.

8. Surjit Singh, *Christology and Personality*, 1961, pp. 166f.

9. Radhakrishnan, Op. cit., p. 159.

10. Adelheid Krämer: *Christus und Christentum in Denken des modernen Hinduismus*, 1958, p. 93: "Als notwendige, spirituelle und soziale Ergaenzung zum wissenschaftlichen Fortschritt dieses Jahrhunderts erscheit ihm die Vereinigung der Religionen in einer Universalreligion, einem 'Commonwealth of Religions'".

11. What Radhakrishnan means by Christ being the spirit of the

Supreme may be known from the following quotation: "Suppose a Christian approaches a Hindu teacher for spiritual guidance, he would not ask his Christian pupil to discard his allegiance to Christ but would tell him that his idea of Christ was not adequate and would lead him to a knowledge of the real Christ, the incorporate Supreme. Every God accepted by Hinduism is elevated and ultimately identified with the central Reality which is one with the deeper self of man. . . . Brahmā, Visnu, Siva, Krsna, Kāli, Buddha and other historical names are used indiscriminately for the Absolute Reality." (*The Hindu View of Life*, p. 46). It is to be noted that the Atman-Brahman concept is also implied in this statement.

12. Cf. Donald T. Rowlingson, *Jesus the Religious Ultimate*, 1961, pp. 4f.
13. Adelheid Kraemer: Op. cit., pp 33f.
14. Ninian Smart, *A Dialogue of Religion*, 1960, p. 83.
15. O. Wolff, *Mahatma und Christus*, p. 26f: "Ob aber die Jesum-Tradition historisch wahr oder nicht, bedeutet mir nichts. Fur mich ist sie wahrer als jede Geschichte, denn sie birst ein ewiges Gesetz, das Gesetz des stellvertretenden und unschuldigen Leidens in seinem wahren Sinne." This saying of Gandhi is quoted in Adelheid Krämer, Op. cit., p. 82.
16. Hu Shih, "Religion and Philosophy in Chinese History", in *Symposium on Chinese Culture*, ed. by S. H. Chen Zen, 1931, p. 25.
17. Wing-tsit Chan, *Religious Trends in Modern China*, 1953, pp. 248f.
18. ibid., p. 174.
19. Cf. Lin Yu-tang, *From Pagan to Christian*, 1959. In my opinion this book should be included in the list of assigned readings for Chinese theological students in South East Asia in the course of their training.
20. ibid., p. 225.
21. ibid., p. 235.
    † See Review in SEAJOT, July 1960.
22. Lin Yu-tang, Op. cit., p. 231.
23. Wing-tsit Chan, Op. cit., p. 176.
24. Francis C. M. Wei, *The Spirit of Chinese Culture*, 1947, pp. 157f.
25. Reinhold Niebuhr, *The Nature and Destiny of Man*, p. 57. Karl Barth puts the same thing in a different way: "The atonement is, noetically, the history about Jesus Christ, and ontically, Jesus Christ's own history. To say atonement is to say Jesus Christ. To speak of it is to speak of His history." (*Church Dogmatics*, 4/1, p. 158).
26. G. C. Berkouwer, *The Person of Christ*, 1954, p. 105: "In the Bible we continually encounter the irrefragable unity of Christ's person and work. . . . Not to know who he is means: not to understand what his work is; and not to see right perspective is not to understand his person." Cf. also H. R. Mackintosh, *The Person of Christ* pp. 321f.

27. Karl Barth has a section in *Church Dogmatics*, 2/1, entitled "The Being of God in Act". The Words "Being" and "Act" can express better the ontological relation of God to his Acts, than the traditional expression "Person and Work". I am indebted to Prof. T. F. Torrance of the University of Edinburgh for an attempt to workout the relationship of "Being and Act" in Christology.
28. D. M. Baillie, *God was in Christ*, p. 52.
29. J. L. M. Haire, in his article called "On Behalf of Chalcedon" in *Essays in Christology* edited by T. H. L. Parker, says in effect: "Clearly it is not his (D. M. Baille's) intention to state an Adoptionist Christology, but his method of approach by beginning with the human experience tends in this direction."
30. D. M. Baillie, Op. cit., p. 70.
31. Nicolas Berdyaev, *Freedom and the Spirit*, p. 189, quoted by Surjit Singh in *Christology and Personality*, p. 101.
32. Surjit Singh, Op. cit., p. 19.
33. Joseph M. Kitagawa, *Religions of the East*, pp. 161f.
34. Paul Tillich, *Christianity and the Encounter of the World Religions*, 1961, p. 61.
35. Cf. Feng Yu-lan, *A History of Chinese Philosophy*, Vol. I, p. 31 and p. 375.
36. "rsis" means the blessed saints, or men who in previous universe have ascended far towards the supreme goal and are therefore especially capable of perceiving divine truth.
37. Swami Prabhavananda, *The Spiritual Heritage of India*, 1962, p. 55.

CHAPTER 6

1. The word "pain" may be translated "Passion", but the translation "pain" links this essay with Professor Kitamori's interest in the theology of the Pain of God. (Translator)
2. K. Holl, *Gessammelte Aufsätze zur Kirchengeschichte*. Munich 1919, Vol. II, pp. 118f.
3. ibid., p. 119.
4. ibid., p. 118.
5. Professor Kitamori indicates here that the colloquial Japanese translation of 1955 uses the more concrete word *itameru* to express the verb; the older version has used a word expressing "grief" or "anguish". (Tr.)
6. The author indicates that the word "suffer pain" expresses a combination of concrete pain expressed by the Japanese verb *itameru* and mental and spiritual anguish expressed by the verb *nayamu*. (Tr.)
7. Kirisutokyo Daijiten, (*Dictionary of Christianity*), Tokyo 1963, p. 521.

8. A reference to the same article on "divine impassibility" in the dictionary. (Tr.)
9. ibid.
10. M. Luther, *Die Schmalkaldischen Artikel*, 1537, WA 30, 3, 87.
11. Masahisa Uemura (1858–1925) in *Reisei no Kiki* (Die Krisis des Geistlichen).